HARRY STYLES

THE UNOFFICIAL BIOGRAPHY

UK | USA | Canada | Ireland | Australia
India | New Zealand | South Africa

Puffin Books is part of the Penguin Random House group of companies
whose addresses can be found at global.penguinrandomhouse.com.

www.penguin.co.uk
www.puffin.co.uk
www.ladybird.co.uk

Penguin
Random House
UK

First published 2017
001

Written by Ali Cronin
Cover and interior design by Nina Tara – ninataradesign.com
Text copyright © Penguin Books Ltd, 2017

Printed in Great Britain by Clays Ltd, St Ives plc

A CIP catalogue record for this book is available from the British Library

ISBN: 978–0–241–33117–0

All correspondence to:
Puffin Books
Penguin Random House Children's
80 Strand, London WC2R 0RL

HARRY
STYLES

THE UNOFFICIAL BIOGRAPHY

PUFFIN

CONTENTS

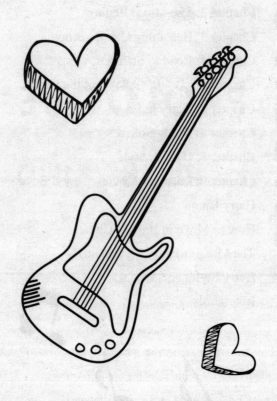

PROLOGUE
WORK HARD, PLAY HARD, BE KIND

Harry Styles didn't have a showbiz upbringing. He didn't have music lessons or dance lessons, and he went to a normal comprehensive school, yet he is now one of the most famous recording artists in the world. He has gone from fronting a band at school to *The X Factor* to huge success with One Direction (aka 1D), and now he's acing it as a solo artist and movie actor. His astronomical rise to stardom can't just be down to his good looks (although, let's face it, they are *good*), and that leads us to the question: what's so special about Harry?

Of his success, Harry told *Another Man* magazine, 'If you can step outside of the craziness and appreciate it for the fact that it's extraordinary, see it as this amazing thing for a second, it's all right. If you just think that's how life is, that's when you lose touch. It's good to have people who can tell you you're an idiot.'

We're not going to call Harry an idiot (the very idea!), but we are totally going to delve into the life of one of the sweetest guys in showbiz; the man whose motto is 'Work hard, play hard, be kind'. What was his childhood like? What kind of teen was he? How did it feel to be on *The X Factor*? Has fame really not changed him at all? And what the heck is it that he loves so much about being naked?!

Let's find out, shall we?

CHAPTER 1
JUST A
NORMAL KID

It was close to midnight on Monday, 31 January 1994. Twenty-six-year-old Anne Styles clutched her bump and panted in pain, while her husband, Des, thirty-five, parked the car as fast as he could at the Alexandra Hospital in Redditch, Worcestershire. At home their little girl, Gemma, who was three at the time, was fast asleep, completely unaware that she would soon have a new baby brother or sister.

Back at the hospital, things were not quite so calm. The midwife took one look at Anne and knew that this was not going to be a long labour. Anne and Des were rushed into a delivery suite where, at six minutes past midnight on Tuesday 1 February, Anne gave birth to a healthy baby boy.

'We only just made it in time!' Des later said.

After some discussion, they settled on the name Harry Edward for their new baby boy.

A retired ambulance worker also called Harry Styles later claimed that Harry was named after him. He told WalesOnline that he had looked after Anne when she felt poorly at a pop concert in Birmingham while she was heavily pregnant with Harry. Apparently, she saw his name badge and said, 'You're quite nice. If it's a boy I'm going to call him Harry.'

Whether that's true or not, it's impossible to think of the Harry Styles we know and love as having any other name: Edward Styles just doesn't have the same ring to it (although we can sort of see him as an Eddie).

Harry was, unsurprisingly, a gorgeous baby. Early photos of him show an almost unbearably cute little boy with straight blond hair and big blue eyes (the dark curly hair and green eyes came later), and a huge, cheeky grin. He was still only a baby when the Styles family moved to Holmes Chapel, a village twenty-one miles south of Manchester.

'That's one of the places where I feel like I disappear the most, if that's what I'm in need of.'

'Not much happens there,' Harry later said during his *X Factor* audition. 'It's picturesque, but quite boring.' Perfect, in other words, for a young family. Even now Harry goes back home if he needs to escape.

'My parents still live where I grew up, so that's one

of the places where I feel like I disappear the most, if that's what I'm in need of,' he told *Another Man*. 'I go back to Cheshire a lot and walk around the same fields, and it's one of the things that isn't going to change, no matter what happens. I'm lucky that I still have a base up there.'

At the age of two, little Harry was enrolled at the local Happy Days Club & Nursery School, where he went while his parents were at work. (Anne worked in an office, and Des worked for financial companies.) As Harry later confirmed in One Direction's book, *Dare to Dream*, 'They were happy days, to be fair.'

By all accounts Harry was a good boy, always smiling, playing with his toys, painting or drawing. At home, while he liked the music that his dad would play – Elvis Presley, Queen and The Beatles, usually – there was no sign at this early stage that he would follow a musical path himself. He was just a normal, smiley kid.

The only inkling that he might have what it took to go far was that he was always willing to try something new. If the caregivers who ran Happy Days suggested a new activity, he would happily join in and do his best. There's also the fact that he was a total charmer from day one – that probably helped. He would even share his dummy with the family dog, a border collie cross called Max. Gross, yes . . . but oh so cute!

When Harry was four he left Happy Days and started in the reception class at Hermitage Primary School. He was a happy, boisterous child, and it was at primary school that his love of performing first began to come to light. On hot days he would entertain the school-run parents by standing up in his seat in the back of the car and performing for them through the open window. This led to a love of acting in school plays, and lead roles beckoned. Would you like to see a six-year-old Harry Styles wearing his big sister's tights and a headband with glued-on ears in one of his primary-school productions? Course you would! Search 'Harry Styles Barney the Mouse' on YouTube and marvel at the cuteness.

This love of performing carried on till the end of his time at Hermitage Primary. In one of his school's newsletters it was noted, 'We all remember Harry for a fantastic performance as the Pharaoh ("Elvis") in *Joseph and the Amazing Technicolor Dreamcoat* in Year 6.'

HARRY FACT

Harry's favourite football team is Manchester United.

'Even then he had that sort of magnetism that made people just want to watch him,' his sister, Gemma, told *Another Man* magazine. 'He made people laugh. Babies still tend to stare at him now – it's kind of weird.'

She also went on to add, 'He didn't find it difficult to make friends.' And he was friends with girls as well as boys.

'I wasn't one of those boys who thought girls were smelly and didn't like them,' he has said. 'I was kind of friends with everyone.'

His first crush was on a little girl called Phoebe – the daughter of one of Anne's friends. Despite the fact that he gave her a teddy bear (cute!), she wasn't interested.

His best mate, Will Sweeny, told the *Daily Star*, 'I've known him since he was four years old. I know it sounds funny, but even in primary school he had a few girls on the go. From Year 4, when he was about ten, Harry started with proper girlfriends. He just had this unbelievable way with girls all his life . . .'

Overall, little Harry seemed to lead a charmed existence.

'He would do what he wanted, but often it seemed that what he wanted was to make other people happy,' said Gemma. Whether this was pretending to be a whole class of students so Gemma could play being the teacher, or getting so overexcited at the prospect of giving his mum a present that he blurted out what she was about to unwrap, he liked to see people smile.

'You wouldn't see him cry . . . but he cried then.'

But Harry's time at primary school wasn't always happy. Behind the scenes, his parents were having troubles. His dad, Des, described what he remembers as 'the worst day of my life' to the *Daily Record*.

'Harry was only about seven when I sat them [Harry and Gemma] down and told them I was leaving,' he said. 'Generally, you wouldn't see him cry as much as maybe some kids do – he wasn't generally emotional or a crybaby – but he cried then.'

For two years after that Des slept in the spare room and the family tried to struggle on, but eventually Harry's parents made the difficult decision to part for good.

'It was quite a weird time,' said Harry in *Dare to Dream*. 'I guess I didn't really get what was going on properly. I was just sad that my parents weren't going to be together any more.'

'Of course, I missed him and Gemma,' said Des. 'It was tough. I used to feed him every night at half ten, change his nappy, put him to bed when he was a baby, and then I was no longer living with them.'

HARRY FACT

As well as his dog, Max, Harry had a pet hamster. Called Hamster. Way to be original, Hazza!

After the split, Anne was briefly married to a man called John Cox, the landlord of a pub in Northwich, Cheshire. The family lived there for a few years, then when Anne and John divorced they moved back to Holmes Chapel, and Harry started in Year 7 at Holmes Chapel Comprehensive School. Gemma remembers Harry's teachers being surprised that this confident, cheeky boy was her brother. While she was painfully shy and a straight-A student, Harry was a joker.

Now a teacher herself, Gemma wrote in *Another Man* magazine, 'He was talkative and very distracting – not ideal for a productive lesson.'

Harry wasn't a bad student, though. He loved sports – especially football (he played in goal for his local Holmes Chapel Hurricanes team), badminton and cricket – and he usually earned Bs for his work, despite a lack of confidence. According to Gemma, he always felt like he had to keep up with her. Anne would often quietly ask Gemma to help Harry revise for exams, because they stressed him out so much.

'I could never fathom how he had a confidence problem,' wrote Gemma. 'I would have traded my As for his Bs and charisma in a heartbeat.'

It was around this time that Anne started seeing a new man: Robin Twist. Harry had always liked Robin, so he was delighted when one evening, while Anne and Robin were watching *Coronation Street*, Robin made the spur-of-the-moment decision to propose. Who needs a romantic location like Paris or New York when you have a sofa, a telly and each other? It's easy to see where Harry gets his down-to-earth attitude from.

Anne and Robin were married in 2013, during a break from Harry's hectic touring schedule with One Direction. Harry was thrilled and honoured when the man who had helped to bring him up from the age of seven invited him to be best man. Anne looked beautiful in a floor-length ivory dress with a bouquet of white roses.

HARRY FACT

Harry is scared of only two things: the dark and snakes.

'He hardly left his mum's side and she looked really proud of him,' a guest told the *Sunday Mirror*. 'He couldn't stop smiling. He sipped champagne and chatted to everyone.'

Making his best-man speech was, Harry said, 'the most nerve-wracking thing I've ever done', but of course he pulled it off, making all the guests both laugh out loud and get teary-eyed, as all good speeches should.

As well as a stepdad, Harry gained a stepbrother when his mum and Robin were married: Robin had a son, Mike, from his first marriage.

'It's what's inside the person that matters to Harry.'

Around the same time that Robin and Anne met and started seeing each other, Harry was also entering the world of relationships.

'I had a few girlfriends here and there when I was really young, but I didn't have an actual girlfriend until I was twelve,' Harry told *The Sun*. 'Then I went out with a girl called Emilie, and for quite a long time considering how young we were. She's still a good friend now.

'I was also with a girl called Abi,' he went on. 'I guess you could say she was my first serious girlfriend.'

Harry's best mate, Will Sweeny, told *Sugarscape*, '[Harry's] girlfriends were long term, for like a year, year and a half. He was dead caring to them too; he'd never cheat or mess them around. He talked about how a girl seemed like a nice person, not what her body was like. It's what's inside the person that matters to Harry.'

When Harry was fourteen he started a Saturday job at a local bakery, W. Mandeville, in Holmes Chapel. As well as serving customers, he would wash the floor, clean up out the back, wash the trays and clean the counter. Every day he would have a brunch pasty (that'll be bacon, cheese and beans. In pastry. The boy has taste) and a cake – definitely one of the perks of working in a baker's – and all day long he would, according to manager Simon Wakefield, charm the customers.

'He was the most polite member of staff we've ever had,' he told the *Mirror*. 'Customers really took a shine to him. The shop suddenly had an influx of girls when Harry worked here. Sometimes there would be twelve of them pouring in at one time.'

According to Simon, everyone in the shop could tell that Harry was going places.

'There was always a good atmosphere when he was around,' Simon told the BBC. 'He used to burst into song in front of the staff. We always knew he had it in him.'

'He used to burst into song in front of everyone. We always knew he had it in him.'

Harry took his GCSEs in the summer of 2010. He did brilliantly, gaining twelve A* to C grades, and he decided to take A levels in Law, Sociology and Business, with a vague plan to become a lawyer.

A certain TV show put paid to that idea, though. Harry didn't know it yet, but the performing, the singing, the charm and the charisma that had been the bedrock of his whole childhood were about to change his life forever . . .

QUIZ

HOW MUCH DO YOU KNOW ABOUT HARRY'S CHILDHOOD?

1. Where was Harry born?

    A. Bromsgrove ☐

    B. Holmes Chapel ☐

    C. Redditch ☐

2. What primary school did Harry go to?

    A. Hermitage ☐

    B. Armitage ☐

    C. Holmes Chapel ☐

3. What was the name of the mouse Harry played in his school production?

    A. Bobby ☐

    B. Barney ☐

    C. Billy ☐

4. How old was Harry when his parents split up?

    A. 4 □

    B. 7 □

    C. 9 □

5. What was the name of the football team Harry played for?

    A. Holmes Chapel Hammers □

    B. Holmes Chapel Houdinis □

    C. Holmes Chapel Hurricanes □

6. What was the name of Harry's first 'serious girlfriend'?

    A. Emilie □

    B. Abi □

    C. Sophie □

7. What did baby Harry used to share with the family dog, Max?

    A. His dummy □

    B. His toy dog □

    C. His bottle □

8. What job did Harry's mum do after they moved to Northwich?

    A. Hotel manager ☐

    B. Pub landlady ☐

    C. Session singer ☐

9. What was the name of Harry's secondary school?

    A. Holmes Chapel High ☐

    B. Holmes Chapel Prep ☐

    C. Holmes Chapel Comprehensive ☐

10. How many GCSEs at grade A* to C did Harry get?

    A. 12 ☐

    B. 11 ☐

    C. 10 ☐

Answers:

1C, 2A, 3B, 4B, 5C, 6B, 7A, 8B, 9C, 10A

Results:

0–4 correct: Out of Styles

Could be better! But don't worry – Harry won't mind.
He's not bothered by this kind of thing.

5–7 correct: Halfway Harry

Not bad! Your Styles knowledge is pretty good. Read the
chapter again and you'll get 10/10, no probs ;)

8–10 correct: Harry High-Five

You are a Styles genius! If there was a GCSE in Harry
Styles: The Early Years, you'd ace it.

CHAPTER 2
THE MUSIC BEGINS

As you know, Harry doesn't come from a showbiz family. He wasn't one of those kids who attended dance classes every day after school and was taken to auditions every weekend. He went to a normal comprehensive school, had a laugh with his mates and sang in the shower or in the car – just like a million other children. The closest he came to making a professional recording was when his granddad, Brian, bought him a karaoke machine and he recorded himself singing Elvis Presley's 'The Girl of My Best Friend'.

HARRY FACT

The first time Harry performed in public was doing karaoke at a pub when he was nine. 'I sang "My Way" by Frank Sinatra and I was not very confident,' he told *Entertainment Weekly*. His performance went down well, but, he said, 'I knew most of the people in the audience so I think they were being nice.'

And that's the clue to his future: singing. Wherever he went, Harry would sing. At work, in the playground, around the house. He wasn't performing or doing it to show off how great his voice was; he was singing for the love of it.

Harry's earliest musical influences came from the music his parents played around the house.

'My dad was a big fan of The Beatles, Elvis Presley, The Rolling Stones, Fleetwood Mac, that kinda stuff,' he told *Entertainment Weekly*. 'I think, if you grew up listening to that, a child can't not be influenced . . . And then my mum was crazy into Norah Jones and Shania Twain, so I have that side.

'I think the first music I bought with my own money was *Bat Out of Hell*,' Harry went on. 'Meat Loaf. I think I was about ten. My mum and dad already had that album that I listened to, and then my dad lost his *Bat Out of Hell* so I went out and got one.'

Harry also loved – and still loves – Coldplay. Their album *Parachutes* came out when Harry was fourteen, and he would listen to it over and over again. (It seems the feeling's mutual. Chris Martin, lead singer of Coldplay, recently told BBC Radio 1's Nick Grimshaw

that he would 'give it all up to run Harry's fan club'.
A man after our own heart.)

'Harry said, "I don't want to sing", but I didn't give him a choice.'

When Harry was in Year 10 his best friend, Will
Sweeny, formed a band with another guy called Haydn
Morris. Will was on drums, and Haydn played the
guitar. They asked Harry to try out to be their bassist,
then discovered that another friend, Nick Clough, could
already play bass. So they recruited Nick instead and
– in a move that, a few years down the line, millions
of fans would thank them for – they asked Harry to be

their singer. And lo, Harry Styles the vocalist was born.

But, actually, it wasn't that easy. To start with, Harry didn't think he was good enough to be a singer. Like most people, he hated listening back to himself.

'It was a week before our school Battle of the Bands contest and we needed a bassist and a singer,' Will Sweeny told the *Manchester Evening News*. 'Me, Harry and Haydn were best friends and we knew Nick Clough, who was starting to play bass. Harry said, "I don't want to sing", but I didn't give him a choice. I pushed him to sing.'

And for that, Will, we salute you.

The band – at this point still nameless – started rehearsing at Will's house. Their influences were rock bands like Blink 182, You Me At Six, Kings of Leon and Green Day, but the tracks they practised to play at the Battle of the Bands competition were 'Summer of '69' by Bryan Adams, and Jet's 'Are You Gonna Be My Girl?'.

But they couldn't enter the competition without a name. The boys had a bit of a brainstorm, each saying anything that popped into their heads. Harry blurted out 'White Eskimo!' and the others liked it – so White Eskimo they were (and still are: they now exist Harry-less and regularly play gigs).

On 2 July 2009, White Eskimo nervously took their place in the school canteen, ready to compete against the eleven other bands in the Holmes Chapel Comprehensive Battle of the Bands. Harry had his first taste of the stage fright that would plague him for years to come, but he and the other boys in the band had rehearsed too much and they were all too excited to even think about backing out now.

Harry needn't have worried. They played a blinder. There was cheering and whooping, and people taking photos; if throwing pants was appropriate in a school setting, who's to say that wouldn't have happened too? It just had that kind of exciting, intense feeling. The judges must have felt it too: White Eskimo won.

'They were really good,' a member of the audience told the *Crewe Chronicle*. 'Everyone was really impressed. We all knew [Harry] could sing, because we could see him singing in the corridors all the time.'

Winning the Battle of the Bands was a huge event for Harry. If he hadn't joined White Eskimo, if they hadn't entered the competition and if they hadn't won, it's highly unlikely that Harry would ever have gone on to audition for *The X Factor*.

'The Battle of the Bands competition showed me that's what I wanted to do. It was such a thrill being in front of that many people, singing. It made me want to do it more and more,' Harry told Dermot O'Leary at his first *X Factor* audition.

'People tell me I'm a good singer. It's normally my mum. Singing is what I want to do.'

Harry's Top Ten All-time Favourite Songs

(as revealed to *Another Man*)

1. Pink Floyd, 'Breathe'
2. Elvis Presley, 'Can't Help Falling in Love'
3. Paul McCartney, 'Heart of the Country'
4. Crosby, Stills & Nash, 'Helplessly Hoping'
5. Ray Charles, 'Drown in My Own Tears'
6. Blaze Foley, 'Ooh Love'
7. Simon & Garfunkel, 'Bridge Over Troubled Water'
8. Van Morrison, 'Tupelo Honey'
9. Travis, 'Flowers in the Window'
10. Patsy Cline, 'She's Got You'

White Eskimo began to practise regularly, playing more school gigs (usually in assembly – beats by about a gazillion miles having to listen to school notices and watch people receive certificates) and even performing at a wedding, where they debuted a song they had written called 'Gone in a Week' and – most importantly – got paid for their troubles. Collecting their wages was pretty much a massive light-bulb above Harry's head: he could sing . . . and get paid for it?! This was a future he could get behind.

But was it realistic? Harry wasn't sure. He thought about auditioning for *The X Factor*, and even talked about it with his fellow band members, but it was more an exciting daydream than something he could see himself actually doing. For a start, at sixteen he was only just old enough to be eligible. For the time being, he focused on revising for his GCSEs and deciding which A level courses to take.

In the end, it was his mum, Anne, who persuaded him to go for it – 'persuaded' as in 'filled in the application form for him' – something for which Harry has said he will always be grateful. He's not the only one. At this point we <3 Anne almost as much as we <3 Harry.

It was decided: he would audition in Manchester. Harry had psyched himself up. This was it – he was actually going to do it. But then, the day before his televised audition, Harry Styles was rushed to hospital. His *X Factor* journey was over before it had even begun.

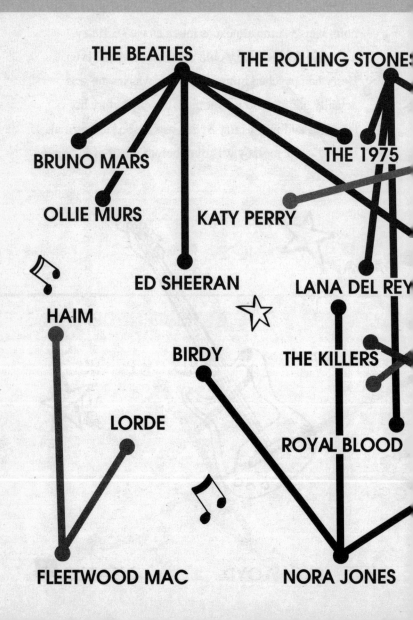

THE BEATLES

THE ROLLING STONES

BRUNO MARS

THE 1975

OLLIE MURS

KATY PERRY

ED SHEERAN

LANA DEL REY

HAIM

BIRDY

THE KILLERS

LORDE

ROYAL BLOOD

FLEETWOOD MAC

NORA JONES

A lot of Harry's musical influences are pretty old-school. To save you the trouble of looking them all up on YouTube, here's a handy guide to getting inside Harry Styles' musical brain . . .

CHAPTER 3
BECOMING
ONE DIRECTION

Spring 2010, just after 3 a.m. Harry Styles was awake and getting dressed. Just like when you have to wake up early to go on holiday, Harry didn't feel tired: just very excited. Harry, his friend Will and his mum arrived at the Trafford Centre in Manchester at around six, ready for the first *X Factor* audition.

'We skived off school and stood in the queue for four or five hours,' Will told the *Manchester Evening News*. 'He auditioned because his mum applied for him and I said, "Of course I'll come with you".'

There are several rounds of auditions before anyone gets the chance to perform for Simon Cowell and the other judges; the *X Factor* production team only let the really good – and the really bad – acts through. It goes without saying that Harry was one of the best, and for his big audition in front of the judges his family had 'We think Harry has the X Factor' T-shirts made (*how* much do we love Harry's fam?!).

But it was so nearly all over before it had even begun. The day before his televised audition, on 10 April 2010, Harry became horribly ill. It was hours until potentially the biggest day of his life, and he was hardly able to stand up, let alone travel to Manchester and sing at an audition.

'I was really ill,' Harry told *Celebs Now*. 'I remember I kept throwing up and then I got really bad and started coughing up blood.'

It got so bad that his worried mum took him to hospital. Eventually, he stopped being sick and was allowed to go home, but the doctors had no idea what was wrong with him.

'They discharged me, but to this day I don't know what it was,' he said.

It was a very close call, but no one who saw Harry at the auditions the next day would ever have guessed how poorly he had been just hours earlier.

If you haven't already looked up Harry's audition on YouTube, do it! Go on, we'll wait . . .

Harry looks young and adorable with his mop of curly hair, slouchy cardi and scarf, and his skin is entirely too perfect for a sixteen-year-old. He looks and sounds utterly calm and confident as he is interviewed by host Dermot O'Leary before his big moment. After being kissed by pretty much everyone in his entire family, Harry walks on to the stage and faces the judges – Simon Cowell, Nicole Scherzinger and Louis Walsh – for the first time.

'This show is designed to find someone like you whether you're fifteen, sixteen, seventeen.'

If you want to see the definition of charisma, just watch Harry Styles walking on to that stage. He hasn't even opened his mouth and already the audience is cheering for him. His audition song was 'Isn't She Lovely?' by Stevie Wonder, which he sang entirely without accompaniment. It was a brilliant audition. He sounded strong, confident and soulful, and backstage his family were practically vibrating with joy; they knew he'd owned that stage.

Nicole Scherzinger was in love. 'I'm really glad that we had the opportunity to hear you a cappella,' she told him. 'We could really hear how great your voice is. For sixteen, you have a beautiful voice.'

But Louis wasn't so sure. 'You're so young,' he said. 'I don't think you have enough experience or confidence yet.'

In the end, though, Simon Cowell shot Louis down and had the final word. 'Someone in the audience just said "rubbish" and I totally agree with them,' he said, referring to Louis' comment. 'This show is designed to find someone like you whether you're fifteen, sixteen, seventeen. It doesn't matter. I think with a bit of vocal coaching, actually, you could be very good.'

Next came the votes.

Harry, bless him, didn't stop smiling as Louis told him that 'for all the right reasons' he was going to say no. The audience booed, Simon booed, even Harry did a very cute little boo.

Nicole and Simon were in total agreement: Harry deserved to go through to boot camp. After a slightly shell-shocked thank you to the judges, Harry walked off stage and into the arms of his very happy, very proud family.

HARRY FACT

Harry deleted his Facebook account after his *X Factor* success, because he had to keep it all a secret until the series was aired on TV and he didn't want his friends posting on his wall about it.

A grand total of 211 people made it through to the boot-camp stage in July 2010. Harry tried not to think about his chances other than to tell himself he had to give this his all. As Simon Cowell told everyone, 'By the end of the day, half of you are going home . . . You're going to sing one song. There are literally no second chances.'

There was also the potential obstacle of Louis Walsh, who was to judge the boot-camp auditionees alongside Simon. Louis hadn't wanted Harry to get through to this round; now Harry had to give him such an amazing performance that he would change his mind. That's a heck of a lot of pressure on someone whose only previous experience was performing in school assemblies and at a local wedding.

First of all, the auditionees were divided into their categories: Boys, Girls, Over Twenty-fives, and Groups. As all the auditions had yet to be shown on TV, no one knew how good their fellow acts were going to be.

Everyone in the Boys group was asked to learn and rehearse Michael Jackson's 'Man in the Mirror'. Since everyone was singing the same song, Harry knew he had to make it his own if he was going to stand out from the crowd. As it happened, the field was narrowed by some of the boys freaking out under the pressure and either fudging the words, the notes or both. Harry did what he needed to do. He made it through to boot camp day two.

Among the other boys joining him on day two were

Louis Tomlinson from Doncaster, Niall Horan from Mullingar in Ireland, Zayn Malik from Bradford and Liam Payne from Wolverhampton. They didn't know each other. Not yet, anyway.

After that first day of boot camp, Harry went back to his hotel. No family or friends were allowed to accompany him at this stage of the competition, so he was on his own. A lot of the auditionees celebrated by getting drunk and staying up pretty much all night, but this competition meant too much to Harry for that. He joined them for a couple of hours, then went to bed.

'I really don't want to go home.'

Boot camp day two began with the announcement from Simon and Louis that the boys were to learn a dance to 'Telephone' by Lady Gaga, featuring Beyoncé. The show's resident choreographer, Brian Friedman, told them they needn't be scared. 'What we are going to work on is your stage presence and choreography,' he told them.

But still, when you're a teenage boy and your only previous experience of dancing is shuffling about to a slow song at the school disco, this kind of thing is very scary indeed. In fact, Zayn was so reluctant to be shown dancing on telly that he initially refused to join in. It took Simon Cowell to talk him down and persuade him to give it a go.

Conversely, Harry turned out to be a natural at dancing; he picked up the routine quickly. He had always been happy to give new things a go and never had that trait been more valuable than right now.

'As you go through boot camp, you kind of realize how big the prize is,' Harry explained in a backstage interview. 'So being here the last few days has made me realize how much I want to stay. I really don't want to go home now.'

On the third day, Nicole Scherzinger joined Simon and Louis on the judging panel. The contestants were given forty songs to choose from for their performance, and Harry chose 'Stop Crying Your Heart Out' by Oasis, because he thought it was a safe option: not too many high notes.

'When I look back on it now, it's really annoying because my performance was so boring,' he later told the interviewer in the TV documentary *One Direction: A Year in the Making*.

Each act performed their song, then left the stage; they had no audience reaction and no idea what the judges thought. Hours later – it must have felt like days – the boys were called back on to the stage. There were thirty of them up there, but only eight would go through. Those were pretty damn scary odds.

As the names of those who were staying were called out, Harry felt sick. He wanted this so badly.

'John Wilding.' One name down.

'Nicolo Festa.' Two.

'Paije Richardson.' Three.

'Aiden Grimshaw.' Four.

'Marlon McKenzie.' Five. Three more chances.

'Karl Brown.' Six. This could still happen – two more names still had to be called.

'Matt Cardle.' Seven. OK, last chance. Harry's heart was practically beating through his chest. Could it be him?

'Tom Richards,' said Simon. 'That's it, guys. I'm really sorry.'

The dream was over. Harry was devastated. 'I'm really gutted,' he said, wiping away tears with his beanie. Niall and Liam gave equally emotional interviews. It was horrendous to have worked so hard and to have got this far, and suddenly it was all over. For Harry it was time to go back to Holmes Chapel and get ready to start in Year 12 that September.

But, just as he was about to collect his things and leave, Harry was called back on to the stage, along with Zayn, Liam, Niall and Louis, and four girls who had also failed to make it through. None of them had any idea what was going on, and none of them dared for a second to believe that they might have been given a second chance. Simon had been pretty clear earlier there would be no second chances for anyone.

'Thank you so much for coming back,' said Nicole. 'Judging from some of your faces, this is really hard. We've thought long and hard about it, and we've thought of each of you as individuals, and we just feel that you're too talented to let go of. We think it would be a great idea to have two separate groups.'

Simon later told *Rolling Stone*, 'Each of [the One Direction boys] individually had very good auditions. We had high hopes for two or three of them in particular, and then it all kind of fell apart at one of the latter stages. Interestingly, when they left, I had a bad feeling that maybe we shouldn't have lost them and maybe there was something else we should do with them. And this is when the idea came about that we should see if they could work as a group. We invited these five guys back. They were the only five we cared about.'

At 8.22 p.m. on 23 July 2010, One Direction was formed. '[I went from] the worst feeling in my life to the best,' Harry later said.

As soon as Simon saw the boys together, he knew

he was on to something. 'The minute they stood there for the first time together, it was a weird feeling,' he told *Rolling Stone*. 'They just looked like a group at that point. I had a good feeling, but then obviously we had about a five-week wait where they had to work together . . . I was concerned whether five weeks was long enough, but they came back five weeks later and were absolutely sensational.'

Harry's *X Factor* journey wasn't even over, but his One Direction journey had already begun.

The One Direction Boys in Brief

Harry Styles

Middle name: Edward

From: Redditch, England

Born: 1 February 1994

First *X Factor* audition song: *Isn't She Lovely?*
by Stevie Wonder

Quick fact: On 1D's album *Up All Night* Harry
has more solo time than anyone else in the
group: over seven minutes.

Zayn Malik

Middle name: Javadd

From: Bradford, England

Born: 12 January 1993

First *X Factor* audition song: 'Let Me Love
You' by Mario

Quick fact: Zayn originally wanted
to be an English teacher

Niall Horan

Middle name: James

From: Mullingar, Ireland

Born: 13 September 1993

First *X Factor* audition song:

'So Sick' by Ne-Yo

Quick fact: Niall is terrified of birds because he was once attacked by one while he was on the toilet. We shouldn't laugh . . .

Liam Payne

Middle name: James (same as Niall!)

From: Wolverhampton, England

Born: 29 August 1993

First *X Factor* audition song: 'Cry Me a River' by Michael Bublé

Quick fact: When he was twelve, Liam took up boxing as a way of dealing with the older boys who were bullying him at school

Louis Tomlinson

Middle name: William

From: Doncaster, England

Born: 24 December 1991

First *X Factor* audition song: 'Hey There Delilah' by Plain White Ts

Quick fact: Liam was an actor and appeared in several TV programmes before auditioning for *The X Factor*

CHAPTER 4
ROAD TO STARDOM

Harry, Liam, Niall, Louis and Zayn existed as a group
. . . but they had no name, they'd never performed in
front of an audience together, and they hadn't had a single
session together with Simon Cowell. Most importantly,
none of the *X Factor* episodes had aired on TV yet, so
there was every chance they could still be dropped before
they'd even begun. They had five weeks to become an
official band, and they had to do this by themselves.

After a few days back at their respective homes, the
boys all met up at Harry's. His family had a bungalow

at the bottom of the garden. It was just one room, but it was big enough for them to bung in a few inflatable mattresses and their stuff. They hung out, played football, swam in the outdoor pool (nice!), ate a shedload of KFC and sang together while Niall played the guitar. In short, they got to know each other.

'You put your differences aside and get on with it.'

Before they even got to Harry's, though, they had wanted to come up with a name for their group. Without a name, they were just five lads hanging out and having a bit of a jam. With a name, they were a band, a unit. As with White Eskimo, it was Harry who came up with the winner.

'Before we met up for the time to practise, we were texting each other names constantly,' Harry told the *Today* show in Australia. 'I kind of thought [One Direction] would sound good when the *X Factor* man said it. So then I texted the boys and they all seemed to like it.'

There were some arguments in those first weeks. These five boys had each wanted to be solo artists, but they'd been thrown together as a group. They all had different personalities, different influences, liked different music, and all wanted to be the lead singer. But at the same time they all knew that this was an opportunity they'd be crazy to let go of. As Liam told Digital Spy, 'You just get over it because you know we're all going for the same thing, so you just put your differences aside and get on with it.'

Liam also told the *Shropshire Star*, 'The dynamic of our band is that there are loud people and there are quiet people, and there are people in between. But we all get on so well, it's unbelievable. Everyone is just so happy to be here . . . It's hard to get to sleep at night – everyone just carries on joking about.'

'This for us is just unbelievable!' Zayn told the *X Factor* website. 'It feels like a dream and that we're all going to wake up and our mums are gonna be like, "Wake up, get ready for school!" kind of thing.'

'My head is saying it's a risk and my heart is saying you deserve a shot.'

The time came for the boys to fly out to Simon's Spanish villa. Harry's bungalow and pool were nothing compared to this £15,000-per-week mansion. There were twenty bedrooms, three swimming pools, a cinema and a gym: more than enough space for all eight groups to stay. It was reported at the time that certain members of certain groups basically trashed the joint, drinking Simon's very expensive champagne and imported beer, and getting sand and water all over the eye-wateringly expensive furnishings. Of course, there was no indication that Harry was involved: Anne, Robin and Des surely brought him up better than that!

'To teach them a lesson, any damage to the villa will have to be paid out of their first royalty cheque – if they make it,' Simon told reporters. In other words, he let them off.

The One Direction boys worked their little socks off, practising their songs over and over again and organizing their look (they decided that all their clothes should be a combination of blue, white and brown). But then disaster very nearly struck when poor Louis was stung on the foot by a sea urchin and had to go to hospital.

'We're all panicking a little bit,' Zayn told the *X Factor* cameras, with Liam adding, 'I hope he's back, as we really do need him.'

He returned just in time, and the boys got ready to wow Simon. (Watch the performance on YouTube and you'll see that Louis is wearing flip-flops – his foot was still sore!) Even though the boys absolutely nailed their version of Natalie Imbruglia's 'Torn', judging by Mr Cowell's face you'd think he was completely 'whatevs' about the whole thing. The boys walked away with no idea how they had done. Simon's only comment was, 'They're cool. They're relevant.'

But in a later interview with *Rolling Stone*, Simon revealed that his 'meh' face totally didn't correspond with what was going on inside his head. 'When they came to my house in Spain and performed [I realized they were going to be huge] after about a millionth of a second. I tried to keep a straight face for a bit of drama for the show . . . They just had it. They had this confidence. They were fun. They worked out the arrangements themselves. They were like a gang of friends, and kind of fearless as well.'

Meanwhile, Harry and the boys had to wait a whole night and half of the following day before they learned their fate. It must have been agonizing!

'Your hunger for it grows and grows as you get

through each stage in the competition,' Harry told the cameras. 'It's just the biggest stage to be told yes or no . . . it's one word that can change your life forever, because it won't be the same if you get a "yes", and if you get a "no" then it's straight back to doing stuff that kind of drives you to come here in the first place.'

When Simon finally decided to put them out of their misery, Harry and the boys stood as one, arms round each other's shoulders.

'My head is saying it's a risk and my heart is saying you deserve a shot,' Simon told them. 'Guys, I've gone with my heart. You're through.'

Harry, with tears in his eyes, basically threw himself at Simon to give the man a hug, closely followed by Zayn, Niall, Liam and Louis. Group 1D hug! (We'd like one of those, please.) Harry could *not* have been happier: they were through to the live shows! He couldn't wait to phone home and tell his family.

The boys had to keep their delight a little bit in check while they were still in Spain and on the plane home, though, as most of the groups hadn't made it through, and they didn't want to make them feel any worse than they already did.

The *X Factor* house was a £3.5 million mansion on the outskirts of north London. It was on a private road surrounded by woodland, and none of the finalists or the production team were allowed to say where it was. Even so, it didn't take long for the press to find it. Luckily, the mass of trees and a couple of 24/7 security guards meant the inhabitants weren't bothered too much by screaming fans.

The 1D boys all lived together in one room. It had wardrobes, two sets of bunk beds and a single bed – and from day one it was a total pigsty. Even their bathroom was disgusting, with pants all over the floor. Mmm, nice . . . not. But, apart from Harry's snoring and sleep-talking, Louis' messiness and an unfortunate food-poisoning incident (poor Harry burst blood vessels in his neck from all the vomming), the boys really bonded – and, anyway, they had a huge job to do. They had to prepare for the live shows and for their first performance: Coldplay's 'Viva la Vida'.

'When we walked in and saw the studio for the first time, then when the five of us stood behind the doors for the first time on the live show, for that first song – for me that was the best moment,' Harry told the *X Factor* website.

By this time, the *X Factor* series had started on TV and Harry's face was becoming known. He was even accidentally knocked over by overexcited fans on his way to the studio one day, but he just struggled to his feet, smiling throughout. He was living the dream; no way was he going to complain about it.

They aced 'Viva la Vida', with judge Dannii Minogue calling them 'the perfect band'. On to week two . . .

HARRY FACT

Harry had to sign an agreement promising that he wouldn't tell anyone other than his family that he had got through to the live shows. Even after the news was leaked to the press, he still couldn't say a word!

Remember the strange unexplained sickness that saw Harry rushed to hospital the day before his first televised audition? It was as if it had come back to haunt him. During the soundcheck for the second live show, when One Direction were due to perform Kelly Clarkson's 'My Life Would Suck Without You', Harry felt so sick he had to sit it out. He was even seen by a doctor. But the *X Factor* bosses thought they knew what was going on: Harry had stage fright. That would certainly explain his earlier sickness.

'I've never had stage fright before that has prevented me performing,' said Harry. And it didn't prevent him this time, either. He swallowed his fear and went out on to that stage and killed it, as always.

'I have to say, you are five heart-throbs,' Dannii told them. 'You look great together and, Harry, whatever nerves you have, I'm sure that your friends and you will stick together.'

Cheryl, another one of the judges, was even more effusive. 'I can't even cope with how cute you are,' she gushed. 'I'm watching the whole time thinking,

This is adorable!'

Even Simon called them 'the most exciting pop band in the country today'. That's the equivalent of a normal non-poker-faced person breaking into full-on tears of joy.

By now, One Direction were becoming well-known by the *X Factor*-viewing public, and Harry in particular was grabbed by fans every time the boys arrived at the studio for rehearsals. Everywhere he went, he was asked for his autograph or a picture.

'It's been a big confidence boost for him,' his mum, Anne, told *Star* magazine – but both his family and the One Direction boys were quick to mercilessly take the mickey out of any band member who started to show even remotely diva-like tendencies.

As the weeks went by, the One Direction boys aced live performance after live performance. As Dannii told them, 'Guys, you are so consistent it's scary.'

But it wasn't just the quality of their singing that was endearing them to the judges; their great attitude and work ethic were also making their mark.

'This is the first time in all the years of *X Factor* where I genuinely believe a group are going to win this competition,' Simon told them. 'You've remained focused, you've been really nice to the crew, you're nice to the fans and, most importantly, everything that happened tonight, from the choice of song to what you wore, it was all down to you. Guys, congratulations.'

It was the day of the live final, and the One Direction lads joined Matt Cardle, Rebecca Ferguson and Cher Lloyd in front of the joyfully screaming audience. This was it! The One Direction boys really thought they were going be *X Factor* 2010 winners, and their excitement was off the scale.

But, of course, they didn't win. They didn't even come second. The boys were gutted, with Harry unable to stop himself crying as he walked off the stage. But, in an echo of the *X Factor* episode where they were canned as solo artists but then suddenly reinstated as a band, Simon Cowell called them into his office and offered them a £2 million recording contract. Third place, schmird place. Talk about an emotional rollercoaster!

'I tried to stay as calm as possible, but on the inside I was terrified,' Harry said in *Dare to Dream*. 'As soon as Simon told us we had a record deal I started crying and I sat there thinking, *Why am I crying? If this works out it's going to totally change my life.*'

The show's winner, Matt Cardle, had only been offered a £1 million contract, so this was a massive vote of confidence from the Cowell-ster.

One Direction had officially hit the big time.

One Direction's *X Factor* Live Songs

Week One: Coldplay, 'Viva la Vida'

Week Two: Kelly Clarkson, 'My Life Would
Suck Without You'

Week Three: Pink, 'Nobody Knows'

Week Four: Bonnie Tyler, 'Total Eclipse
of the Heart'

Week Five: Kim Wilde, 'Kids in America'

Week Six: Elton John, 'Something About the Way You Look Tonight'

Week Seven: The Beatles, 'All You Need is Love'

Week Eight: Bryan Adams, 'Summer of '69' and Joe Cocker, 'You Are So Beautiful'

Week Nine: Rihanna, 'Only Girl in the World' and Snow Patrol, 'Chasing Cars'

Week Ten: Elton John, 'Your Song', Robbie Williams, 'She's the One' and Natalie Imbruglia 'Torn'

CHAPTER 5
1D – IT'S ALL ABOUT THE FANS

O ne Direction are going to be big,' PR expert Mark Borkowski told *Star* magazine. (PR stands for public relations – all the celebs have PR people on board to make sure they get lots of positive press and online coverage.) 'They'll definitely be millionaires by this time next year . . . Harry is already a cult figure. It's all there for them.'

It was the beginning of a massively exciting time for Harry and the boys, and it started in style, with Simon giving them £8,000 (EIGHT THOUSAND POUNDS!)

pocket money each. (Simon, if you're reading, we've always loved you. Those trousers suit you – who wants a cold stomach? – and your hairstyle is awesome. Just saying.)

So, with their bank accounts bulging like never before, the 1D boys headed home for Christmas. Harry hung out with his friends, watched festive telly, and signed autographs and chatted to fans whenever they approached him.

'It's all about the fans,' he told radio station The End. 'They're incredible, so everything we do is for them.'

The 1D lads knew that part of Simon's faith in them came from the amazing reaction from their fans, and the boys swore they would never take their fans for granted.

The year 2011 kicked off with a trip to Los Angeles for meetings with producers and to make a start on recording some tracks. The boys had an amazing time and met some amazing people, but it was their welcome when they stepped off the plane when they got back to the UK that really blew them away. Literally hundreds of screaming fans stood between the boys and the exit, while paparazzi photographers took photo after photo. It was madness, with girls leaping on the boys in a frenzied attempt to touch some 1D flesh. Clothes were ripped, hair was pulled, and in the end the police were called and the boys had to leg it into a riot van. Bear in mind that at this point they had released precisely no music! It was enough to blow the mind of a boy from a small town in Cheshire – especially when the 1D management team decided that the only way to ensure the boys didn't get screaming-fan-related injuries was to employ a team of bodyguards.

Harry turned seventeen on 1 February 2011, and soon afterwards the boys started rehearsals for their thirty-seven-date *X Factor* live tour. They had to learn choreography and a new song: 'Forever Young'. This was the track they would have performed had they won *X Factor* – somehow we think that particular disappointment had somewhat faded in the light of their record deal, their time in LA, and so on . . .

The boys bloomin' loved the tour, performing in huge arenas to thousands of fans who screamed with joy and waved One Direction banners, then going back to their dressing room, where they could mess about, play jokes on each other and generally have a mahoosive laugh. Harry loved every second of it.

The newspaper reviews were less than complimentary – but then newspaper journalists aren't exactly the 1D target audience, so WHO CARES! The *Daily Telegraph* reviewer wrote, 'The main draw for the girl-dominated crowd were Cowell-mentored boy band One Direction. Hysterical screams greeted their every move. Hyperventilating ensued when they ran through the crowd. When cheekily cherubic heart-throb Harry Styles danced to the front, squeals reached fever pitch.' See, *that's* what had always counted to the boys, and always would: the response of the fans.

After the tour, the boys were allowed some time off for a well-earned break. Harry and Louis went skiing in Courchevel in the French Alps. They had become properly close over the previous few months and genuinely loved hanging out together. (Who could forget the massively cute T-shirt Harry wore during one of the book signings for *Forever Young*, which had HARRY HEARTS LOUIS emblazoned across the front?) Although they were asked for photos or autographs by a few fans while they were in France, it turned out they weren't quite as well known over there as they thought.

'One time Harry and I were skiing together when a girl and a guy came up to us with a camera,' Louis told *Seventeen*. 'We assumed they were going to ask us for a photo, so we stood there with our arms round each other, posing. They said, "No, we want you to take a photo of us!" It was embarrassing.'

HARRY FACT

Harry once tweeted that he fancied a doughnut. Result: he was sent doughnuts. Now that's what we call the power of social media!

Up All Night Track Listing

'What Makes You Beautiful'

'Gotta Be You'

'One Thing'

'More Than This'

'Up All Night'

'I Wish'

'Tell Me a Lie'

'Taken'

'I Want'

'Everything About You'

'Same Mistakes'

'Save You Tonight'

'Stole My Heart'

'Stand Up' (Bonus track on the
Deluxe edition)

'Moments' (Bonus track on the
Deluxe edition)

After their time off, it was all systems go to actually release some music. While the boys had been on the *X Factor* tour, several songwriters had been working on tracks for the first One Direction album – including the boys' vocal coach, Savan Kotecha (he had already written hits for Westlife, Britney Spears, Usher and others), Kelly Clarkson and Ed Sheeran, no less. The boys recorded the album in Sweden, the UK and the US, working with a variety of producers.

'We worked really hard on the first album to find the right songs,' Harry says in *Dare to Dream*. 'We wanted our first single to be a big summer song. For instance, when The Black Eyed Peas' single 'I Gotta Feeling' came out in 2009, it was the song of the summer. When everyone heard it, it reminded them of all the good times they'd had. We wanted our first single to be like that and be the song that everyone would remember.'

The boys decided that song should be 'What Makes You Beautiful'. It was released in September 2011 and took a weeny fifteen minutes to reach number one on iTunes. It sold 153,965 copies in its first week alone (for comparison, the average single has to sell about 100,000 copies to get to number one). They had shot the video on a beach in Malibu, California, over two days in July 2011. In the video, the boys act out, meeting up with three girl friends on the beach. Harry is in love with one of the girls, who doesn't know she's beautiful. Watch the video and you'll see Louis driving a camper van. Apparently he was so nervous he drove at a snail's pace, leading to them being pulled over by the police. Twice. Bless, Louis!

'This is such a feel-good track, we'd be amazed if it doesn't go straight to number one,' said CBBC's *Newsround*, while the *NME* reviewer said, 'The real genius is that the chord progression is simple enough to be played on an acoustic guitar at a house party.'

Despite all this, Harry's stage fright was still rearing its ugly head. In their first TV performance as a signed band, on ITV's *Red or Black?*, his hands were shaking and he was visibly scared. He even lost his voice during his solo lines. He was properly gutted that he had, in his mind, let the rest of the group down. He even googled

'Harry's s**t' and read all the negative comments people had written about him. Doubtless if he'd searched 'I love Harry Styles' he'd have seen positive comments instead, but that's not how our minds work when we feel like we've messed up. And, as he said in the TV documentary *One Direction: A Year in the Making*, 'If there are three people saying you're amazing you don't think, *Why are they saying I'm amazing?* They say I'm amazing 'cause they're a fan. But if there is one saying they hate me, *Why do they hate me? What have I done?* . . . I can definitely take criticism but it is just like a "I don't like you". I want to know why people don't like me.' Poor Harry.

Trooper that he is, though, this didn't put him off singing live on their promotional radio-station tour. 'What Makes You Beautiful' did well (understatement!) worldwide, reaching number one in Ireland and Mexico, number two in New Zealand, number three in Japan, and so on. It was an international mega hit by anyone's standards, and has to this date sold well over five million copies.

More singles from the album followed, as well as a world tour. One Direction had existed for less than two years, but they already had a number-one album, several hit singles, and had performed live to massive crowds in Sweden, Germany, France, Italy, Holland, Australia, New Zealand, Mexico, the US and Canada. Not winning in *The X Factor*, in fact, coming third, must have seemed like a distant memory. The money was starting to roll in, and the boys were able to drop a cool few million pounds on buying their own houses and new cars.

Harry loved his new life, but he also loved going home to Holmes Chapel on the rare occasions that he had time off from the very hectic 1D schedule. He hung out with his friends and was the same Harry he'd always been, but he started getting abuse from some people who had been to his school or who lived in his town but didn't even know him. They would swear at him or shout insults at him. It was upsetting for poor old Haz, because it wasn't like he was swanning around holding a HA HA I'M RICH AND FAMOUS

AND YOU'RE NOT! banner or brandishing fistfuls of tenners. He was also starting to get trolled online.

He was still only just eighteen at this point, so it was hard for him. As Zayn told *The Sun*, 'It does annoy us a bit. He's a young kid and people are just giving him grief for no reason.'

The other side of this was the abuse that any woman seen with Harry received – and still receives – on social media. His hairdresser and bezzie mate, Lou Teasdale, got so much abuse when a photo of her and Harry went viral that she closed her Twitter account. Lou and Harry have never remotely been an item – she has a partner and a child! It's totally weird that people troll women who Harry likes – not just because it's a disgusting thing to do, but also because by doing so the trolls themselves have made damn sure that Harry dislikes them intensely.

Harry and the 1D boys have a love–hate relationship with social media. While they hate the trolls, they love the effect that platforms like Twitter, YouTube, Tumblr and Facebook had on their initial success. On their *Up All Night* tour, they were greeted by hordes of screaming fans even in the countries where they were yet to release 'What Makes You Beautiful'. That was all down to social media.

'It's really important that we connect directly with our fans through the likes of Twitter so they can get to know us,' Harry told the *Guardian*. 'There'd be no point someone in the office doing it, because that would defeat the object . . . If it wasn't us on the thing, the fans wouldn't know us.'

Simon Cowell agreed, telling *Rolling Stone*, 'The band has to make it happen by themselves. I think that's what One Direction did. We worked as a partnership, but without their input and the way they spoke to the fans and the kind of people they are, it wouldn't have happened in the way that it's happening now.'

'As much as we were the biggest, most famous boy band in the world, it felt weird.'

Over the next three years 1D went from strength to strength. They released the albums *Take Me Home*, *Midnight Memories*, *Four* and *Made in the A.M.*, selling millions of copies worldwide. They played concerts all over the world and won about a kajillion awards, including six Brit Awards, four MTV Video Music Awards, eleven MTV Europe Music Awards, seven American Music Awards (including Artist of the Year in 2014 and 2015), and twenty-seven (!) Teen Choice Awards. For those three years they lived the dream. But as time went on, one of the 1D boys just wasn't feeling it in the way that he did at the beginning. That boy was, of course, Zayn.

'I wasn't one hundred per cent behind the music. It

wasn't me,' he later told US blogger Perez Hilton. 'It was music that was already given to us, and we were told "this is what is going to sell to these people". As much as we were the biggest, most famous boy band in the world, it felt weird.'

He signed off citing stress while the group were touring Asia, then on 25 March 2015 he left One Direction. It was a shock move to Harry and the rest of 1D but, as Zayn later told Perez Hilton, 'I woke up on that morning, if I'm being completely honest with you, and was like, "I need to go home. I just need to be me now, because I've had enough."'

One Direction's management released a statement saying, 'After five incredible years Zayn Malik has decided to leave One Direction. Niall, Harry, Liam and Louis will continue as a four-piece and look forward to the forthcoming concerts of their world tour and recording their fifth album, due to be released later this year.'

In reality, the band were devastated, and mere hours after Zayn's announcement Harry was filmed in floods of tears on stage, while Louis put his arm round an imaginary Zayn. One Direction had been a five-piece through five years of hard work, joy and success. Harry couldn't believe that his friend wanted to walk away from that.

It was only five months after Zayn's departure that the rest of the group decided to take a break. Harry later told *Rolling Stone*, 'I didn't want to exhaust our fan base. If you're shortsighted, you can think, *Let's just keep touring*, but we all thought too much of the group than to let that happen. You realize you're exhausted and you don't want to drain people's belief in you.'

One Direction may have finished (for the time being), but Harry was under no illusions about how much he owed Simon Cowell and his bandmates. 'I love the band,' he said. 'The band changed my life, gave me everything.'

B'bye, 1D . . .

Hello, Harry Styles, solo artist.

1D in Numbers

45 weeks spent in the UK Top 10
singles chart

4 number-one singles

Around 50 million albums sold worldwide

£25 million: estimated wealth of each member of 1D
(according to the 2015 *Sunday Times* Rich List)

4 out of 4 albums entering the US charts
at number one – the first band EVER
to do this!

CHAPTER 6
HARRY IN LOVE

Harry Styles is known as much for his girlfriends as for his music. Every time he's photographed with someone of the opposite sex the press assumes they're dating. He's a lovely man with a lot of friends, and it'd be physically impossible for him to have dated every woman he's ever been photographed with. But that's not to say he hasn't had his share. Like we said: he's a lovely man.

Harry says he doesn't have a 'type' as such. 'It's more about the person. How they act, their body language, if they can laugh at themselves,' he said in an interview

HARRY
STYLES

THE UNOFFICIAL BIOGRAPHY

Harry arriving at *The X Factor* finals, November 2010

The X Factor finalists,
December 2010

Harry at the
Nickelodeon Kids'
Choice Awards in LA,
March 2012

London Fashion Week, London, September 2013

One Direction play in a charity football match, Leicester, May 2014

Appearing on *NBC's Today Show* to mark the release of 'Four',
Florida, November 2014

© Gareth Cattermole / Staff / Getty Images

© Olivia Salazar / Getty Images

Harry attends a dinner to celebrate the launch of a TOPMAN collection, London, June 2015

One Direction perform on stage at the KIIS FM Jingle Ball 2015, LA, December 2015

Harry performing in New York, May 2017

Harry performs on *The Late Late Show with James Cordon*, LA, May 2017

Harry performs for SiriusXM Live at The Roxy Theatre,
West Hollywood, May 2017

Harry performs on *The Late Late Show with James Corden*, LA, May 2017

with *Cosmopolitan*.

Let's find out, shall we? Here, for your reading pleasure, are (some of) Harry's relationships. You're welcome.

Caroline Flack

It's probably safe to say that Harry's rep as a ladies' man started in 2011. He was seventeen and TV presenter Caroline Flack was thirty-two. He'd made no secret of the fact that he fancied her, commenting on the *X Factor* website, 'If Caroline Flack is reading this, say "Hi" from me. She is gorgeous!' and he told the *Daily Star Sunday* that he thought she was 'hot'. Meanwhile, Caroline tweeted, 'Watching one direction in chattyman ... Is Harry Styles the cutest thing you've ever seen?' To which Louis replied, 'You don't know how happy this will make Harry hahaa.' So there was flirting on both sides. Here were two people who already knew they fancied one another.

Then, at an *X Factor* party in October 2011, partygoers saw Harry make a beeline for Caroline. They chatted . . . and then they kissed. Pretty audacious for a seventeen-year-old, but Harry had always been confident in that way. Remember the teddy bear he gave his friend Phoebe when he was five?! Anyway, so far, so pretty standard for a seventeen-year-old at a party. The only issue – in some people's eyes – was the fifteen-year age gap. Harry wasn't even old enough to drink alcohol, and here he was being photographed sharing a cab with a woman in her thirties. (At this point, by the way, Harry's own mum was still in her thirties!)

Harry and Caroline managed to keep their relationship under wraps for a couple of months, with Harry dropping the odd hint in interviews about liking older women and fancying Caroline. Then Harry was papped leaving Caroline's house at 9.30 in the morning, and their secret was out.

To say some of Harry's fans weren't best pleased is a huge understatement. Twitter was awash with teenage girls throwing shade at Caroline. 'If Caroline flirts with my boyfriend [Harry] I will personally hunt her down and shoot her,' said one. 'I want to kill you, Caroline

Flack,' said another. 'Harry is mine, b***h.'

In response, Caroline dignifiedly tweeted, 'I'm close friends with Harry. He's one of the nicest people I know. I don't deserve death threats.' In an interview with *Now* magazine she said, 'What's hard for me to get my head around is people saying it's disgusting. I don't think it is. Harry told me, "Don't listen to Twitter." He became the mature one at that point. I was like, "I know, but it's still quite hurtful."'

Apparently it wasn't just the fans who weren't impressed with Harry and Caroline's relationship. A source told *Star* magazine that Harry's mum wasn't thrilled either. 'Anne doesn't want Harry to end up getting hurt. Caroline is a worldly woman who is never short of male attention. Anne just feels Harry needs to stick to girls his own age and says Caroline should back off!' Although this 'source' might have got their wires crossed, as Anne later told the *Mirror* that she'd 'never really thought whether [the relationship] would be a problem'. She went on, 'Personality is more important than anything else. I think the younger you are, the more people will make of an age gap. If Harry was twenty years older, there wouldn't be an issue. My husband was ten years older than me and it didn't bother me one way or the other.'

In the end, Harry and Caroline (Haroline? Carry?) didn't last long. The couple decided to go their separate ways in January 2012, as Harry embarked on his tour with 1D. It wasn't a bad breakup, though, with Harry tweeting, 'This was a mutual decision. She is one of the kindest, sweetest people I know. Please respect that.'

Lucy Horobin

In mid-2012 the press reported that, before Caroline, there had been radio DJ Lucy Horobin. Another thirty-two-year-old, Lucy had interviewed the 1D boys for the Manchester radio station she worked for. They reportedly had a brief fling while Lucy and her husband were going through a rocky patch in their marriage. According to the *Daily Mail* Harry and Lucy's relationship was 'an open secret' at the radio station. They flirted live on air, with Harry telling Lucy that she 'looked lovely'. Sadly, Lucy and her husband later split, with her husband putting the blame firmly at Harry's door. Meanwhile, a close friend of Harry's told the *Mirror*, 'To [Harry] it was clear Lucy had separated from her husband. He had no idea she was still married.'

After the press got wind of the fling and splashed it over their front pages, Lucy was trolled mercilessly on Twitter by 1D fans. She ended up deleting her Twitter account. (Those 1D fans who troll any woman Harry or his bandmates are involved with are bloomin' horrible. Sorry (not sorry), but they are.)

Emma Ostilly

It is thought that Harry met American model Emma when she appeared in the video for 1D's second single 'Gotta Be You'. They were both eighteen at the time. A few months later, Harry visited her in her new home in New Zealand and they were photographed kissing. Cue those mean trolling 1D fans flooding her Twitter account with horrible messages.

Someone who saw the couple chatting in a bar told

the *Sunday Mirror*, 'They really seemed to have a connection and only had eyes for each other . . . They were enjoying themselves, laughing and joking together. They seemed very happy and relaxed and you could tell they have a history together.'

Harry responded to the rumours by saying, 'She's just a friend. She's working over here . . . I prefer not to talk about it.'

Nicole Scherzinger

Nicole was, of course, a judge on *The X Factor* when Harry was a contestant. She claims it was her idea to put Harry, Liam, Niall, Louis and Zayn together as a band (although Simon insists it was his idea), and Harry had always looked up to her. Then in 2013, when Harry was nineteen and Nicole thirty-five, they hooked up. That, maths fans, is a sixteen-year age gap – even more than the gap between Harry and Caroline! However, it seems that Nicole and Harry weren't an item as such, with an insider telling *The Sun*, 'Yes they did snog and got on well, but they never dated.'

Emily Atack

The Inbetweeners actor had a fling with Harry in 2012, but she made her feelings known as early as 2010. She tweeted while watching *The X Factor*, 'Does Harry from One Direction HAVE to be sixteen?! Let's pretend he's eighteen at least! Then there'd be only One Direction he'd be going – to the bedroom!' Blimey!

Later on she told *Reveal* magazine, 'Yeah, we had a short-lived thing. But we were never boyfriend and girlfriend. Harry and I had fun, then went in opposite directions. We haven't spoken in a while.'

Caggie Dunlop

The *Made in Chelsea* star and Harry had a flirtation/ fling in 2012. A showbiz source told the *Mirror*, 'It was obvious Harry had a bit of a thing for Caggie because he started tweeting her before they had ever even met. And when they actually saw each other in person they hit it off straight away. There was obviously real chemistry between them. They swapped numbers and stayed in touch, but nothing happened at first . . . [Then] Harry and

Caggie met up on an evening out and ended up kissing.'

All of which goes to show that, if you want to know who Harry's dating, you need a 'showbiz source' . . .

Taylor Swift

Where do we START?! So, Taylor and Harry met backstage at the 2012 Kids' Choice Awards, with Taylor seen singing and dancing along to 1D's performance of 'What Makes You Beautiful'. Then Justin Bieber naughtily stirred the pot when he told the *Mirror* that 'one of the biggest artists in the world thinks Harry is so hot, but I've been sworn to secrecy'. (Some people think he was talking about Rihanna, mind.)

'She's a really lovely girl. Honestly, she couldn't be a sweeter person,' Harry said of Taylor to *Seventeen* magazine. 'She's a great girl and she's extremely talented . . . she's one of those people you meet [who's] genuinely a nice person. Some people you meet and they are not as nice as you make them out to be, but she's one of those people who's really just amazing.' Gushing, much?

Then Taylor dropped a massive hint that there might be more to their relationship, after she was papped wearing a silver paper-aeroplane necklace identical to one Harry had been photographed wearing.

Finally, on only their second date, Taylor and Harry were papped walking through New York's Central Park.

'When I see photos from that day I think, *Relationships are hard, at any age*,' Harry told *Rolling Stone*. 'And adding in that you don't really understand exactly how it works when you're eighteen, trying to navigate all that stuff didn't make it easier. I mean, you're a little bit awkward to begin with. You're on a date with someone you really like. It should be that simple, right? It was a learning experience for sure. But at the heart of it I just wanted it to be a normal date.'

Harry and Taylor were photographed together all the time during their short relationship. 'It felt very fragile, it felt very tentative,' said Taylor during a performance at the GRAMMY Museum. 'And it always felt like, "OK, what's the next road block? What's the next thing that's gonna deter this? How long do we have before this turns into just an awful mess and we break up? Is it a month? Is it three days?"'

It was three months. They broke up after a big argument while they were on holiday. Poor Hayler.

Taylor's songs 'Out of the Woods' and 'Style' are almost certainly about Harry, and it seems likely that 'Perfect' – a song Harry co-wrote for 1D – is about Taylor, since it contains the lyrics, 'And if you like cameras flashing every time we go out, and if you're looking for someone to write your breakup songs about, baby, I'm perfect'. We'd say it is too!

'I write from my experiences; everyone does that,' Harry told *Rolling Stone*. 'I'm lucky if everything [we went through] helped create those songs. That's what hits your heart. That's the stuff that's hardest to say, and it's the stuff I talk least about . . . Certain things don't work out. There's a lot of things that can be right, and it's still wrong. In writing songs about stuff like that, I like tipping a hat to the time together. You're celebrating the fact it was powerful and made you feel something.'

Harry's Famous Girl Mates

(NOT Girlfriends!)

Cara Delevingne

Lou Teasdale

Pixie Geldof

Alexa Chung

Daisy Lowe

Kimberly Stewart

The model and daughter of gravel-voiced old rocker Rod Stewart apparently hooked up with Harry after he went out for dinner with her, Rod and Rod's wife, Penny Lancaster. How do we know? Because, in a moment of pure embarrassing-dad genius, Rod revealed all to Alan Carr on *Chatty Man*.

'His [Harry's] car was here in the morning, let's put it that way. But he may just have come round to pick something up . . . I've let the cat out of the bag. Harry couldn't be kinder. He is a very funny guy.'

Paige Reifler

Harry and American model (another one!) Paige were papped kissing in 2014. Paige also told the *Mirror* that they'd hooked up. 'Yes, I am seeing him,' she said. Cue – you guessed it – rage from the crazy 1D Twitter trolls, with one tweeting, 'Are you dating Harry or not. That's the only thing we want to know and when we don't get answers we kill.' Terrifying on so many levels.

Nadine Leopold

Harry dated Nadine, a Victoria's Secret underwear model, for a while. Apparently she was constantly worried that he would cheat on her. This along with the fact that they lived a plane ride apart meant their relationship didn't last long.

Kendall Jenner

Harry and Kendall had an on-again off-again relationship between 2014 and 2016. It seemed to mostly revolve around holidays, with the couple first spotted skiing in California in 2014.

'They were very cute together,' a source told People. com. 'There was a lot of flirting and smiling going on.'

Then, in December 2015, they were papped on holiday in Anguilla and St Barts, eating dinner together and messing about on yachts.

At the time, Kendall's sister Khloe Kardashian told *Entertainment Tonight*, 'Do I think they're dating? Yes. I don't know if they're like boyfriend-girlfriend. Nowadays, I don't know, people are weird with stuff.

So I don't know their "title". But, I mean, they were in St Barts together, hanging out, so to me that's dating. I would call that dating.'

Then in September 2016, Harry and Kendall were spotted on a dinner date in LA, with an onlooker saying that the model 'was beaming' all night. 'They're rekindling their old romance and Kendall's so excited and happy about it,' the source told *People*.

And now? One of those handy showbiz sources told HollywoodLife.com, '[Kendall] wouldn't go back to dating Harry again even if he begged her.' So that'll be them off again, then . . .

Tess Ward

Food blogger, chef, author and – you guessed it – model Tess was introduced to Harry by mutual friends in May 2017. A source told *The Sun*, 'As soon as Harry met Tess there was an instant spark between them. They really bonded over their mutual love of quirky fashion and food – and things turned romantic quickly. They've been on a number of dates while Harry has been in London and he's already introduced Tess to some of his close friends, including his personal stylist, Lou Teasdale. This really seems different to Harry's past relationships as Harry genuinely is besotted with Tess and doesn't want to risk messing this one up.'

Naturally, this was like a red rag to the 1D trolls, but this time as well as the usual Twitter stuff they also started leaving scathing one-star reviews for Tess's book on Amazon. One of Harry's saner fans tweeted, 'It's "fans" like that that make us all look like nutballs. It's so childish.' Yup.

Does Harry Have a Type?

Harry has said that he goes for personality
over looks (and age!), but even so: *does* he
have a type? We did the research so you
don't have to. Of the relationships listed above:

64% have blue eyes

64% have blonde hair (and **86%**
of those have long hair)

64% work as models

ALL about the personality, is it Harry?

CHAPTER 7
GOING SOLO

After One Direction started their break, Harry kept a pretty low profile. He was still papped out and about with his friends and girlfriends, but he didn't give any interviews or court any publicity. It later turned out that he had been a very busy bee indeed, planning his first solo album and launching a movie career, no less. The little boy who loved to try new things had never gone away, it seems.

'I loved [being in One Direction] and it was what I wanted,' Harry told *Another Man*, adding in an interview with *The Sun*, 'The thing that I'm happiest about is that I didn't leave [1D] in a place of "I feel so suppressed". I never felt like I was faking it. I really enjoyed it. It's the best thing that ever happened to me.' And, while he has said he would never rule out a One Direction reunion, it's pretty clear that for now he's having a great time doing his own thing. There is also the fact that he left One Direction's management company in February 2016 . . . 'I'm enjoying writing at the moment, trying new things,' he told *Another Man*. 'I've been asking myself, "What do I want to say?"' In April 2017 we found out, when Harry released his first solo single 'Sign of the Times', a totally anthemic, high-noted, harsh-throated slice of glam soft rock. Listen to it once and you find yourself warbling, 'THE BULLETS!' for the rest of the day.

In an interview with *Rolling Stone* Harry said, 'The song is written from a point of view as if a mother was giving birth to a child and there's a complication. The mother is told, "The child is fine, but you're not going to make it." The mother has five minutes to tell the child, "Go forth and conquer."'

Basically it's about coming to terms with the bad things that can happen in the world and making sure you live your life to the full – a sentiment we can all get behind. Also: choon!

HARRY FACT

When Harry first played his album to his mum, she cried. Aw!

'Sign of the Times' was followed a month later by Harry's debut solo album, niftily titled *Harry Styles*. Of this album, he told *The Sun* that he wanted to use his songwriting as a way of exploring love in all its forms, as well as his feelings and emotions about his time with One Direction. 'I found it really therapeutic to write,' he said. 'Sitting at an instrument, you allow yourself to be vulnerable in a different way to speaking to anyone, even

if you know them really well. I found it to be therapy –
things that I'd either not thought about for a long time or
hadn't processed really because things had been moving
so fast. I wanted to put out a piece of me that I haven't
put out before . . . It's really hard to go from doing a
show with thousands of people there to your hotel room
– from being around people to nothing. After five years
of doing that, I learned a lot about myself. There's no
textbook telling you how to go through that stuff.'

Harry's main purpose for the album was to be honest.
'I hadn't done that before,' he told *Rolling Stone*.
'I don't think people want to hear me talk about going
to bars and how great everything is. The champagne
popping . . . who wants to hear about it?' he went on.
'I don't want to hear my favourite artists talk about all
the amazing s**t they get to do. I want to hear, "How
did you feel when you were alone in that hotel room,
because you chose to be alone?"'

Harry Styles: Track Listing

'Meet Me in the Hallway'

'Sign of the Times'

'Carolina'

'Two Ghosts'

'Sweet Creature'

'Only Angel'

'Kiwi'

'Ever Since New York'

'Woman'

'From the Dining Table'

Harry certainly wasn't scared to get vulnerable.
Lyrics like 'Played with myself, where were you? I fell
back to sleep and got drunk by noon, I've never felt less
cool' (from final track 'From the Dining Room Table')
make you want to give him a cup of tea and a cuddle.
'From the Dining Room Table' is his favourite track on
the album, by the way. 'It's just personal, and I don't
feel like I've written a song like this before,' he told
American radio station NPR.

'I've never felt this vulnerable putting out music, because I don't think this is a piece of myself I've put out there before.'

Overall, the album sounds totally non-1D, but that isn't to say Harry is rejecting his roots or turning his back on the music that made him famous. Far from it. In one of our favourite Harry quotes EVER, he told *Rolling Stone*, 'Who's to say that young girls who like pop music – short for popular, right? – have worse musical taste than a thirty-year-old hipster guy? That's not up to you to say. Music is something that's always changing. There's no goal posts. Young girls like The Beatles. You gonna tell me they're not serious? How can you say young girls don't get it? They're our future. Our future doctors, lawyers, mothers, presidents; they kind of keep the world going. Teenage-girl fans – they don't lie. If they like you, they're *there*. They don't act "too cool". They like you, and they tell you. Which is sick.'

YES, HARRY!

Harry has said that he loves listening to his own album. 'I'm really proud of it and I've worked really hard on it,' he told talk-show host Graham Norton. In an interview on The Hits Radio he said, 'I wanted to make songs that I liked, and I wanted to write an album that

I wanted to listen to, and that was kind of all I really wanted to do.'

He also told NPR, 'I've never felt this vulnerable putting out music, because I don't think this is a piece of myself I've put out there before. And, simple fact: When there are other people around you, you share the good stuff – but you also get to share the bad stuff and hide behind everyone else a little bit. So with this, yeah, it is scary. But I think it was time for me to be scared. And I'm still very much learning. And I'm having the time of my life working this out.'

He started writing the album in February 2016, then stopped for five months to make his first movie (more on that later) and finished writing in December 2016. 'I like the writing part the most,' he told BBC Radio 1's Nick Grimshaw, adding that he and his co-writers wrote thirty full songs before choosing their favourites for the album. The album was recorded mostly in Jamaica, as Harry wanted to get away from all his usual influences.

Harry originally wanted to call his album *Pink*, because 'it's the only true rock 'n' roll colour'.

'I didn't know what my own voice was; I didn't know what might happen,' he told NPR. 'So it was really important to me that the only voice really was mine. I felt like if I stayed around places where I knew I was going to have people tell me what they think it should be . . . I knew I was just going to get distracted and frustrated.'

After a new single and an album pretty much always comes the tour, and Harry was no different. Starting in San Francisco in September 2017 and finishing in Tokyo on 8 December the same year, taking in twenty-nine dates in the UK, Canada, France, Germany, Sweden, Holland, Italy, Singapore, Australia and New Zealand, the tour is a big un. But the venues? Not so much. Harry could have sold out the world's major arenas no probs, but instead he purposely chose smaller locations for his concerts.

'I'm really excited to be playing these venues,' he told The Hits Radio. 'It's nice during a show to be able to have conversations with people.'

The only slight (totally massive) problem with playing smaller venues is that, when you're Harry Styles and the whole world loves you, your tour tickets sell out in about two seconds. People were NOT happy, with fans tweeting that they were 'heartbroken' and blaming 'fake fans' (whatever they are) for taking all the tickets. Harry responded by sweetly tweeting ('sweeting'?), 'I am overwhelmed, thank you. If I don't get to see you this tour, I'll come back around next year if you'll have me. Love, H.' Uh, yeah, we think we'll have you, H.

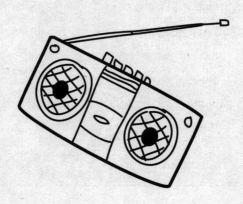

QUIZ

IS YOUR PERSONALITY MORE 1D HARRY OR SOLO HARRY?

1. Do you like the music your parents like?

A. Some of it's pretty good ☐

B. No way! Their taste sucks ☐

C. Yeah, but don't tell anyone ☐

D. Yeah, I listen to it all the time ☐

2. Which kind of music do you like best?

A. Pop ☐

B. Rock ☐

C. Old-school ☐

D. I like them all ☐

3. What's your fave retro decade for music?

A. 1990s

B. 1980s

C. 1970s

D. 1960s

4. What's your fave kind of film?

A. Comedy

B. Romantic comedy

C. Slushy romance

D. Animated

5. Which patch would be your fave to iron on to your jeans?

A. A unicorn

B. A peace sign

C. A skull

D. An emoji

6. What's your fave finger to wear a ring on?

    A. Fourth

    B. Third

    C. Thumb

    D. First

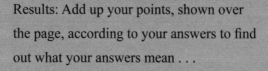

Results: Add up your points, shown over the page, according to your answers to find out what your answers mean . . .

1. A)3 B)2 C)1 D)4

2. A)1 B)2 C)4 D)3

3. A)1 B)2 C)4 D)3

4. A)1 B)4 C)3 D)2

5. A)1 B)3 C)4 D)2

6. A)1 B)4 C)2 D)3

6–12 points: 1D 4eva

You are 1D through and through! You love pop music
and keeping up with the latest crazes (we totally bet you
have a fidget spinner), and you're loyal to what you love.

13–18 points: Styles Chameleon

You loved 1D, you love solo Harry, and what's more you love loads of other kinds of music too. You're not bothered about belonging to any particular tribe. You just like what you like.

19–24 points: Solo Harry for You

You've always been more of a Harry fan than a 1D fan, and you <3 him even more since he went solo. His music is so you!

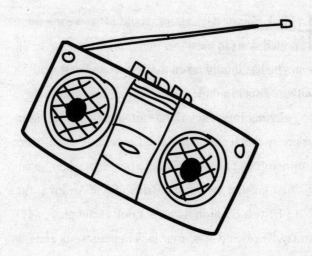

CHAPTER 8
HARRY'S STYLE

In his *X Factor* days Harry would often wear a long knotted scarf to show his individuality, and over the years he has totally taken that theme and galloped with it. This is a dude who bloomin' loves dressing up, whether in a fancy floral suit, a rakish Gucci shirt or pretty much anything Saint Laurent. It's totally not surprising that he was still only nineteen when he won his first fashion award: the British Style Award at the 2013 British Fashion Awards. Look at old pics of 1D and quite often it'll be four lads in plain suits and one in a shall we say *non*-plain suit. Hazza's individual sense of style is what set him apart from other boy-band popsters when he was in 1D, and now that he's a solo artist his fash goes with his music like custard with apple crumble: great on their own, but even better together.

'I always love being comfortable,' he told *The Sun*. 'You should wear what makes you feel comfortable. It's a really good opportunity to have fun – it's clothes; it's not a big deal. It's a good time to express yourself and have fun with it. It's one of those things that you shouldn't take seriously. If you want to wear a pair of yellow trousers you can wear a pair of yellow trousers.' (Is it just us who has a sudden urge to wear yellow trousers?)

HARRY FACT

Harry's number-one fashion tip is 'Make sure it's clean'. We will, Harry, we will.

It's not just about the clothes, either. Harry's hair has had a style evolution all of its own, from the curly man-bob in the early days to the flowing locks of the late-1D days to his latest crop, which he did for that film role.

'I was, like, the one with the long hair,' he says in the Apple Music documentary *Harry Styles: Behind the Album*. 'I'd had it for so much of One Direction. Cutting it off just felt very much like starting afresh.'

He donated his lopped locks to the Little Princess Trust, a charity which provides real-hair wigs for kids who lose their hair due to cancer treatment. What a dude!

The man behind the crop is hairstylist Anthony Turner '[Harry's] jaw dropped to the floor,' Anthony told *Vogue* of the moment he chopped off Harry's ponytail. 'His parents were there,' he went on. '[Harry's mum] was like, "Is that all you're going to do?" She wanted him to be neatened up.' Luckily, Harry soon got into the idea of having short hair. 'He was very articulate and he knew what we were trying to achieve,' said Anthony. 'He's a cheeky, quintessential Brit boy – an absolute pleasure to work with.'

The first photo of Harry's new do pretty much broke the internet, with Twitter divided between those who mourned the loss of his long hair ('Don't like Harry Styles short hair at all, bring back the long mess') and those who embraced the chop ('Harry Styles with short hair makes me feel things'). Frankly, we reckon Harry could carry off any kind of hairstyle. As Anthony said, 'He's a very handsome boy'.

Get the Look

Harry goes for an androgynous look (a bit boyish and a bit girly), which is lucky 'cause it means everyone can copy him. Winning! Here's how . . .

Hair: curly, messy, just got up. This is not a style for gloss spray or straighteners. Add a bandana, beanie or fedora for extra Harry points.

Tops: a fitted tee (roll the sleeves up a couple of times), a loose-fitting shirt in a bright floral or Hawaiian design, a blazer and a couple of long chains or pendants. Done.

Bottoms: Harry does love a suit, so trousers to match the blazer always work. Otherwise black or grey skinny jeans. Obvs.

Shoes: Black ankle boots, cowboy boots or Converse sneakers will do nicely.

Hands: Lots of chunky rings. Check out market stalls for some cheap and cheerful ones.

Add a couple of temporary tattoos and a long floaty scarf, and you're good to go.

NOTE: Harry loves his individual style, so don't feel you need to slavishly copy him. Following your own path is just as Harry-ish as skinny jeans and ankle boots are!

We can't talk about Harry's style without discussing his tattoos. He's got bloomin' loads of the things, from the huge to the mini. At the time of writing he has a mahoosive sixty-one known tats, including some that he regrets.

'I regret this one on my wrist here,' Harry told *We Love Pop,* referring to a tattoo on his left wrist of a small padlock that Ed Sheeran designed and tattooed for him. 'There are some that my friends have done and some that are just awful,' he went on. TBH it's kind of easy to guess which ones he's not mad keen on now. Some are more like doodles you'd do on your workbook when you're bored in class than pieces of body art, but hey-ho, he's an international rock star – it's not like he's going to get turned down for a job because of his tats.

Here's a rundown of Harry's tattoos as of mid-2017, complete with space at the end for you to fill in details of all the new ones he gets in the future. Because, let's face it, he will.

Left upper arm: a star + 'NY LA LDN' + a black heart

Left underside arm: 'Won't stop till we surrender' + 'PINGU' + an iced gem

Left bicep: 'Hi' + a clothes hanger + American football team Green Bay Packers logo + a fern + a skull playing card + 'silver spoon' + an anatomical heart + 'Arlo'

Left upper forearm: 'A' (as in Anne, for his mum. Aw!)

Left forearm: a Bible (covering an old tattoo that said 'I can't') + 'R'

Left hand: a cross

Left wrist: an anchor (covering an old tattoo that said 'I can't change') + a padlock + a key + a shamrock + an Aquarius symbol + '99p'

Left upper torso: an empty birdcage + comedy and tragedy theatre masks + 'SNCL' + two tiny crosses above the initials 'M' and 'K'

Torso: Two swallows + a butterfly + half a heart

Left collarbone: '17BLACK' + 'Love' banner

Left ankle: 'Never gonna'

Right ankle: 'dance again' + a plus sign

Right big toe: a crown

Left shoulder: 'Gemma' in Hebrew, for his sister. Aw times two! + a guitar

Right shoulder: 'G'

More left arm: logo from Pink Floyd's album *The Dark Side of the Moon* + 'Can I stay?' + a ship + a handshake + three nails + a rose + a mermaid + 'YOU BOOZE YOU LOSE' and a bottle + 'Late Late' + 'Jackson' + a bee/fly

Right collarbone: '1957' (Dad's year of birth)

Left collarbone: '1967' (Mum's year of birth)

Left and right hips: laurels (covering an old tattoo that said 'Might as well')

Left upper thigh: 'Brasil!'

Left thigh: a tiger

Right arm: an eagle (covering an old tattoo that said 'Things I can')

Add any new tattoo info here.

When and where did he get it?	Where is it on his body?

What is it?

CHAPTER 9
MUSIC TO MOVIES
. . . AND BEYOND

So you've won a national talent competition, you've been one-fifth (and then a quarter) of the world's biggest boy band, and you've had a number-one solo album. What's next? Movies, obvs! It wasn't long after One Direction started their break that Harry started auditioning for film roles.

'I did acting at school. It's something I've always wanted to explore, but I was busy with the band so I never felt like I had time to do it the right way,' Harry told *Another Man*. 'When we took some time off,

I thought I'd see if it might work. It's a challenge, but it feels good to be out of my comfort zone.'

It seems the powers that be had already been courting Hazza for Hollywood. Big-shot Hollywood producer Harvey Weinstein told *The Sun*, 'When you meet him, he's super charismatic. He came to our Oscars party last year and then I went out to lunch with him. I've met him two or three times and he was very interested and charming. I think the guy is a movie star . . . You know, he's a dashing rogue – a fun-loving, spirited kind of actor that used to be in England all the time . . . We offered him a part and he couldn't do the movie because he had the [One Direction] tour. The amount of money their tour did is crazy, so he's got obligations.'

'I auditioned literally thousands of young men . . . And he had it.'

So it's not very surprising that it wasn't long before Harry was able to tick 'Get role in a blockbuster movie' off his bucket list. In February 2016 it was announced that Harry had been cast in the war epic *Dunkirk*, written and directed by Christopher Nolan (two times Oscar-nominated director of The Dark Knight trilogy, *Inception* and *Interstellar*).

The film tells the story of the Dunkirk evacuation in 1940 during World War II, when 400,000 British, French and Belgian troops found themselves surrounded by the German army on the beaches of Dunkirk, France. Thousands and thousands of soldiers were killed, but the outcome was one that the wartime UK Prime Minister Winston Churchill called a 'miracle'.

'If this evacuation had not been a success, Great Britain would have been obliged to capitulate [give in],' Christopher Nolan told French film magazine *Premiere*. 'And the whole world would have been lost, or would have known a different fate: the Germans would undoubtedly have conquered Europe.'

While lots of Americans don't know the story of

Dunkirk (there were several tweets along the lines of 'What even *is* a Dunkirk?' when Harry's casting was announced), pretty much everyone in Britain has heard of it – if you haven't learned about it at school yet, you soon will do. Add to this the fact that big-name actors such as Tom Hardy, Mark Rylance, Sir Kenneth Branagh and Cillian Murphy are in *Dunkirk*, and it all equals a pretty amazing film role for Harry. He must have been well excited to go for it . . .

Cynical types might assume that Harry just had to rock up to a meeting, say 'Hi, I'm Harry Styles' and flash his cheeky smile to get a part in a film, but cynical types would totes be wrong: Harry had to audition just like everyone else.

During his research, Christopher Nolan found out just how young and inexperienced the soldiers at Dunkirk were, so he decided to cast young and inexperienced actors. Cue Harry Styles.

'We really wanted unknowns,' Christopher told the *Los Angeles Times*. '[Harry is] not that unknown, but he'd never done anything as an actor before. So he auditioned. I auditioned literally thousands of young men with different combinations of young men. And he had it.'

The film's casting director, Jon Papsidera, told *GQ*, 'Harry was absolutely right for the role. As an actor he is unknown, but his readings made him an obvious choice. We thought he was fresh and interesting and he won the role. I don't think he studied acting professionally and yet he won the role against some very well-known actors. He read for me, then us collectively in London. He did half a dozen readings, coming back and forth and it was no easy task for him.'

When asked if Harry had been reluctant to cut his hair for the role of a soldier, Christopher Nolan said, 'I don't want to get into it.' Which kind of proves that he didn't cast Harry for any other reason than his suitability for the part. (Also we can't imagine that any young actor with a movie role would keep that role for long if he started moaning to the director about having a haircut.)

HARRY FACT

Harry had to have his own personal bodyguard on the set of *Dunkirk* to protect him from all the fangirl and fanboy attention.

Harry plays a young soldier stuck on the beach. The trailer shows his character flailing desperately in the sea, while Nazi warplanes swarm overhead – which of course then spawned about a gazillion online stories of the 'DOES HARRY DIE IN *DUNKIRK*?' kind. You probably know by now whether he does or not, but we're not in the business of giving spoilers so you'll have to watch the film to find out . . .

Harry has charmed pretty much everyone he has ever worked with, and his co-stars were no exception. Mark Rylance, a hugely well-respected film, TV and theatre actor, said, 'He's just so positive, brave and brilliant. He's a remarkable young man. There are a lot of remarkable young men in the film . . . I can see why people are very fond of him.'

Meanwhile, Sir Kenneth Branagh, who has done basically every Shakespeare play it's possible to do and received a knighthood to boot, said, 'I think he's very impressive. Very, very impressive.' Like Mark Rylance, he also went on to say that all the boys in the film were very impressive. Harry was just one of the cast; only special if his acting was special (which it totally was).

'Harry Styles is great,' Cillian Murphy told *Radio Times*. 'I had very few scenes with Harry but we got to hang out, and I've got to say he's a great, great kid and really, really funny . . . Above all, Chris Nolan knows talent and would have cast Harry for a reason.'

Dunkirk was filmed in France, Holland, the US and the UK. Harry was used to travelling, of course, after his touring days with 1D, but everything else about the film-making process was totally new to him, and he was pretty scared his first day on set. '[It] was so cold, there was sand in my eyes, it was intense,' he told *Another Man*. 'The movie is really ambitious. It just shocked me how big the whole process is . . . Even just walking in to get lunch and seeing hundreds and hundreds of people sitting around makes you realize the scale of it all.

He also told *Rolling Stone*, 'Some of the stuff they're doing in this movie is insane. And it was hard, man, physically really tough, but I love acting. I love playing someone else. I'd sleep really well at night, then get up and continue drowning.' (Spoiler alert? We're not telling!)

'He has huge star potential and would give the project enormous publicity.'

So what next for Harry the movie star? Oh, nothing much. Only, y' know, THE BIGGEST MOVIE FRANCHISE EVER FROM ONE OF THE BIGGEST STUDIOS EVER! Yes, Disney bosses – that's *the* Disney – apparently seriously considered casting Harry as the young Han Solo in one of the Star Wars – that's *the* Star Wars – instalments. OK, so they didn't actually cast him, but according to *The Sun* Disney are 'keeping tabs on him for future high-profile movies'. A source told the newspaper, 'Harry was one of the early names in contention when the studio looked at Han Solo. Even though he had virtually no acting experience, they saw he had huge star potential and would give the project enormous publicity.'

That 'huge star potential' combined with the real-life actual acting experience he got while filming *Dunkirk* means that the only way is up when it comes to Harry Styles' movie career – as long as Harry himself is up for that, of course. He told BBC Radio 1's Nick Grimshaw that he'll only do more films if he really loves the project.

So – phew! – we don't have to wave b'bye to 'Harry Styles, solo songster' just because he's doing a bit of 'Harry Styles, movie star' stuff. We like Harry multitasking, thanks very much. With a stratospheric solo music career, songwriting credits on tracks by artists like Ariana Grande, Meghan Trainor and Kodaline, and now movie acting, Harry already has a professional life that most sixty-year-olds would be proud of. Who knows what the next forty-odd years will bring for this super-talented, super-lovely twenty-something? We can't bloomin' WAIT to find out!

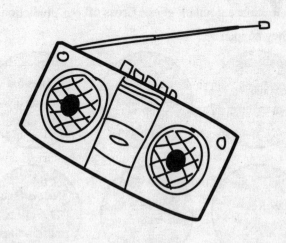

HARRY BINGO

We don't know what's next for Hazza, but we can
have a good ol' guess. Cross off our predictions
as they happen . . .

Gets married

Has a baby

Gives his baby a rock-star name

Writes a musical

Plays one of Shakespeare's major roles on the London stage

Does a One Direction reunion tour

Wins a lead role in a movie

Has a fling with a movie co-star

Finishes a relationship to start one with a co-star

Wins a Grammy

Puts his name to a range of ankle boots

Starts his own fashion label

Has a daughter and gives her the middle name Anne

Does some catwalk modelling

Stars in a West End musical

Gets his own UK chat show

Takes over from James Corden as presenter of *The Late Late Show* in the US

Has a girlfriend in her forties

Becomes Sir Harry Styles

Is awarded an OBE

HOW TO MOVE IN HARRY'S CIRCLES

Harry isn't actually a huge fan of Twitter – hardly surprising, considering the bashing some of his friends and girlfriends get. As he told BBC Radio 1's Nick Grimshaw, 'I don't like saying stuff for the sake of it. There's a lot of nice stuff on Twitter, but there's also a lot of not-nice stuff. If Twitter was a house party, I probably wouldn't go.' And he isn't one of those people who feels lost without his phone. 'Sometimes I'll purposely put [my phone] away,' he told Nick Grimshaw. 'When I was doing my album I'd go, like, three days without [it].'

But he *is* on Twitter, and Instagram. We all love Harry; that's a given. But we're not his *actual friend* (however much we may daydream about it). Next best thing to being his actual friend? Having the same virtual friends as him! So, just for you, we've found the Twitter and Insta accounts of as many of Harry's friends and associates as we can. Go forth and follow! (And be nice: Harry hates trolls.)

And for more online Harry Styles stuff (because the more, the merrier), you can try the following:

TWITTER	INSTAGRAM
@Harry_Styles (if you don't already follow the man himself)	@harrystyles
HARRY'S FAMILY	
@MrsAnneTwist (mum)	@annetwist
@robintwist (stepdad)	@twist_robin_
@desstyles (dad)	@desstyles
@GemmaAnneStyles (sister)	@gemmastyles
@Mike_Selley (uncle)	(not on Instagram)
@Dee_Selley (aunt)	@dee_selley
@matty_selley (cousin)	@matty_selley
@Concept_Ben (cousin)	@concept_ben
@Ella1D (cousin)	@ellaselley

TWITTER	INSTAGRAM
1D (AND ZAYN)	
@LiamPayne	@liampayne
@Louis_Tomlinson	@louist91
@NiallOfficial	@niallhoran
@zaynmalik	@zayn
HARRY'S FRIENDS AND GIRLFRIENDS	
(Some of these accounts are protected due to all the trolling they've had. MAN, we hate trolls)	
@grimmers (Nick Grimshaw)	@grimmyradio1
@carolineflack1	@carolineflack
@LucyHorobin	@lucyhorobin
@emmaostilly	@emmaostilly
@edsheeran	@teddysphotos
@Adele	@adele
@EmAtack	@emilyatackofficial
@Caggie_Dunlop	@caggiesworld
@coldplay	@coldplay
@taylorswift13	@taylorswift
@RitaOra	@ritaora
@henryholland	@henryholland
@Caradelevingne	@caradelevingne
@louteasdale	@louteasdale
@pixiegeldof1	@pixiegeldof
@alexa_chung	@alexachung
@daisylowe	@daisylowe
@kimberlystewart	@thekimberlystewart
@reifpiage	@reiflerpaige
@NadineLeopold	@nadineleopold
@KendallJenner	@kendalljenner
@TessWard	@tessward

TWITTER	INSTAGRAM
HARRY'S HOLMES CHAPEL FRIENDS	
@whiteeskimouk (his old band)	@whiteeskimouk
@WillSweeny	@willsweeny
@AlexMasnyk	@alexmasnyk
@HCGoss ('Holmes Chapel Gossip')	(not on Instagram)
THE X FACTOR	
@TheXFactor	@thexfactor
@SimonCowell	@simoncowell
@CherylOfficial	@cherylofficial
@radioleary (Dermot O'Leary)	@radioleary
@DanniiMinogue	@danniiminogue
@NicoleScherzy	@nicolescherzy
HARRY'S WORKMATES	
@MeghanTrainor	@meghan_trainor
@Kodaline	@kodaline
@ArianaGrande	@arianagrande
@JKCorden (James Corden)	@j_corden
@JeffBhasker (album producer and co-writer)	@jeffbhasker
@TylerSamJ (Tyler Johnson, album co-writer)	@tylersamj
@SalibianMusic (Alex Salibian, album co-writer)	@alexsalibian
@kidharpoon (album co-writer)	@kidharpoon
@JohnHenryRyan (album co-writer)	@johnhenryryan
@HarveyWeinstein	(not on Instagram)

THE MASSIVE HARRY
STYLES QUIZ!

PROVE HOW MASSIVE A FAN YOU ARE! IT'S
NOT EVEN MULTIPLE CHOICE! AND NOT ALL
THE ANSWERS ARE IN THIS BOOK! SQUEAL!

So, yeah. Grab yourself a pen and get answering. (Actual
answers start on page 170 . No peeking, OK?)

1. When exactly did Harry, Niall, Zayn, Liam and Louis become a band?

2. And at what time of day?

3. Where was Simon Cowell's house when Harry was on *The X Factor*?

4. Where did One Direction come in *The X Factor* final?

5. What kind of cake did Harry take as a gift for the band Fleetwood Mac to one of their concerts?

6. What was the song that Harry sang at a pub karaoke night when he was nine?

7. What was the first album that Harry bought with his own money?

8. What's Harry's all-time favourite song, according to an interview he gave in *Another Man* magazine?

9. Who is Harry's childhood friend Will Sweeny's TV-presenter mum?

10. When was Harry's first *X Factor* audition?

11. And what song did he sing?

12. Which *X Factor* judge gave Harry a 'no' after his
first audition?

13. What's the name of the *X Factor* choreographer?

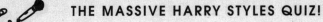

14. What was the 1D boys' takeaway of choice while they were staying at Harry's house during *X Factor*?

15. What colour was the onesie Harry liked to wear while he was living in the *X Factor* house?

16. Along with 1D, who were the other *X Factor* finalists?

17. How much pocket money did Simon give each of the boys after he'd signed them?

18. How long after it was released did 'What Makes You Beautiful' reach number one in the UK singles chart?

19. When did Zayn leave 1D?

20. What was the estimated wealth of each member of
1D when the band took their break?

21. When did One Direction start their break?

22. How old was Caroline Flack when she and Harry
started seeing each other?

23. And how old was Harry?

24. Where were Taylor Swift and Harry photographed on their second date?

25. Which of Taylor's songs are reportedly about her relationship with Harry?

26. Which is Harry's favourite song from his debut solo album?

27. What's Harry's number-one fashion tip?

28. Harry got most of his tattoos in what year?

29. What did Harry get while filming *Dunkirk* that none of the other actors got?

30. When did Harry start writing his solo album?

31. Harry has two of what kind of bird tattooed on his chest?

THE MASSIVE HARRY STYLES QUIZ!

32. And what insect is tattooed underneath the birds?

33. Which tattoo, designed by Ed Sheeran, has Harry said he regrets?

34. Who said he would 'Give it all up to run [Harry's] fan club'?

35. How old was Harry when he won his first award for his sense of style?

36. Which Andrew Lloyd Webber musical did Harry perform in during his final year at primary school?

37. Who did Harry call 'one of the most talented dudes I know'?

38. When did Harry finish writing his first solo album?

39. What role in a Star Wars film was Harry considered for?

40. A fan has put up a sign in LA marking the place where Harry . . . what?

41. What did Sir Kenneth Branagh call Harry's performance in *Dunkirk*?

42. What's the name of Harry's hairstylist?

43. What's the name of Harry's hairstylist's daughter?

44. Which of Harry's exes is the song 'Two Ghosts' apparently about?

45. How many songs did Harry write or co-write for his solo album?

46. Who wrote and directed *Dunkirk*?

47. What did Harry do with the hair he had cut off when he went short?

48. What's Harry's sister's Twitter handle?

49. What colour was the suit Harry wore when he first performed 'Sign of the Times' on TV in the US?

50. What non-Harry Styles songs did Harry sing with James Corden on *Carpool Karaoke*?

Answers:

1. 23 July 2010
2. 8.22 p.m.
3. Marbella, Spain
4. Third
5. Carrot cake
6. 'My Way' by Frank Sinatra
7. *Bat Out of Hell* by Meatloaf
8. 'Breathe' by Pink Floyd
9. Yvette Fielding
10. 11 April 2010
11. 'Isn't She Lovely?' by Stevie Wonder
12. Louis Walsh
13. Brian Friedman
14. KFC
15. White
16. Matt Cardle, Rebecca Ferguson and

Cher Lloyd
17. £8,000
18. Fifteen minutes
19. 25 March 2015
20. £25 million
21. March 2016
22. Thirty-two
23. Seventeen
24. Central Park
25. 'Out of the Woods' and 'Style'
26. 'From the Dining Room Table'
27. 'Make sure it's clean'
28. 2012
29. A personal bodyguard
30. February 2016
31. Swallows
32. A butterfly
33. A padlock

34. Coldplay's Chris Martin

35. Nineteen

36. *Joseph and the Amazing Technicolor Dreamcoat*

37. Ed Sheeran (in a BBC Radio 1 interview)

38. December 2016

39. Young Han Solo

40. Vommed

41. 'Very, very impressive'

42. Lou Teasdale

43. Lux Atkin

44. Taylor Swift

45. Thirty – he then chose his fave ten to go on the album

46. Christopher Nolan

47. He gave it to a charity that makes real-hair wigs for kids with cancer

48. @GemmaAnneStyles

49. Pink

50. 'Hey Ya!' by OutKast, and 'Endless Love' by Diana Ross and Lionel Richie

HARRY STYLES
AND YOU

Harry has always said it's all about the fans – well, here's your chance to make your mark as a true HS fan. Fill this in, keep it safe, remember it always . . .

My favourite Harry hairstyle:

My favourite Harry-on-*X-Factor* moment:

My favourite Harry vocal moment:

My favourite Harry lyric:

My favourite track on the album *Harry Styles*:

My favourite outfit of Harry's:

Person who I think owes Harry an apology:

Person who I think Harry should never let go:

Harry's cutest personality trait:

Three-word review of Harry's performance in *Dunkirk*:

What I think Harry would like best about me:

My ideal scenario for meeting Harry:

My favourite ever Harry moment:

The best thing about Harry:

My favourite pictures of Harry:

stick your pictures
in the frames!

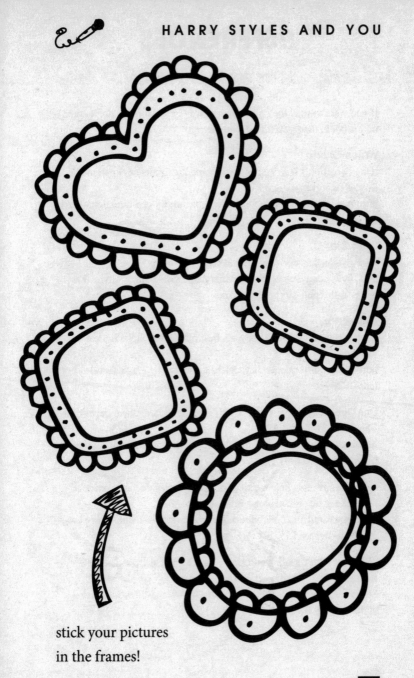

stick your pictures
in the frames!

REFERENCES

If you want to read the online interviews / news stories / etc., quoted in this book, then you'll find them at . . .

Wales Online
'One Direction's Harry Styles was named after me' says paramedic from Newport
http://www.walesonline.co.uk/news/wales-news/one-directions-harry-styles-named-7013310

Daily Star
Harry Styles has been on the pull since he was six
http://www.dailystar.co.uk/showbiz/goss/289272/Harry-Styles-has-been-on-the-pull-since-he-was-six

The Mirror
Harry Styles all smiles as he does best man duties at his mum's wedding
http://www.mirror.co.uk/3am/celebrity-news/harry-styles-smiles-best-man-1926940

One Direction movie: Harry Styles gets job in hometown bakery for This Is Us 3D film
http://www.mirror.co.uk/3am/celebrity-news/one-direction-movie-harry-styles-1871781

1D's Zayn reveals he's worried for Harry Styles, feeling homesick and getting sick racial abuse on Twitter
http://www.mirror.co.uk/3am/celebrity-news/zayn-malik-interview-on-perrie-twitter-1357529

"It's over with Caroline and Harry hasn't got a girlfriend at the moment," says One Direction star's mummy
http://www.mirror.co.uk/3am/celebrity-news/one-directions-harry-styles-mum-821460

Haunted by Harry: Husband couldn't bear to see One Direction singer's face after DJ wife's affair
http://www.mirror.co.uk/3am/celebrity-news/harry-styles-and-lucy-horobin-affair-1111341

When Harry met Caggie! Harry Styles is dating Made in Chelsea's Caggie in weirdest celebrity hook-up of the year
http://www.mirror.co.uk/3am/celebrity-news/harry-styles-dating-caggie-dunlop-1136166

Who's Harry's mystery admirer? Justin Bieber reveals he has a famous friend who fancies One Direction heartthrob
http://www.mirror.co.uk/3am/celebrity-news/justin-bieber-harry-styles-from-one-781851

One Direction's Harry Styles caught kissing a beautiful American model
http://www.mirror.co.uk/night-copy/one-directions-harry-styles-caught-802057

Harry Styles' girl: "I am seeing him" - model ex Paige Reifler says romance is back ON
http://www.mirror.co.uk/3am/celebrity-news/harry-styles-girl-i-am-3904629

Daily Mail
So just what is it about older women, Harry?
Teenage One Direction star had fling with ANOTHER 32-year-old
http://www.dailymail.co.uk/tvshowbiz/article-2164210/One-Direction-star-Harry-Styles-18-fling-radio-presenter-Lucy-Horobin-32.html

People

Harry Styles and Kendall Jenner hit the slopes together
http://people.com/celebrity/harry-styles-and-kendall-jenner-hit-the-slopes-together/

Hollywood Life

Kendall Jenner and Harry Styles' awkward run in – wouldn't date him again if he begged
http://hollywoodlife.com/2017/01/29/kendall-jenner-over-harry-styles-kings-leon-run-in/

The Guardian

One Direction make transatlantic pop history with US No 1 album
https://www.theguardian.com/music/2012/mar/21/one-direction-us-no1-album

Celebs Now

One Direction's Harry Styles: I had my first girlfriend at 12
http://www.celebsnow.co.uk/celebrity-news/copy-of-one-direction-s-harry-styles-i-had-my-first-girlfriend-at-12-100667

One Direction's Harry Styles: I was coughing up blood before my X Factor audition
http://www.celebsnow.co.uk/celebrity-news/one-direction-s-harry-styles-i-was-coughing-up-blood-before-my-x-factor-audition-106507#2GC9s75mT6uIMsDP.99

Caroline Flack my girl? Harry Styles claims: I'm single
http://www.celebsnow.co.uk/celebrity-news/copy-of-harry-styles-claims-i-m-single-106352

Perez Hilton

Zayn Malik opens up about why he really left One Direction
http://perezhilton.com/2015-11-17-zayn-malik-first-major-interview-since-leave-one-direction-fader

Rolling Stone
Exclusive Q&A: Simon Cowell on One Direction's Rise to Stardom
http://www.rollingstone.com/music/news/exclusive-q-a-simon-cowell-on-one-directions-rise-to-stardom-20120409

Harry Styles' New Direction
http://www.rollingstone.com/music/features/harry-styles-opens-up-about-famous-flings-honest-new-lp-w476928

The Sun
One Direction: Chart stars in their own words
https://www.thesun.co.uk/archives/bizarre/784751/one-direction-chart-stars-in-their-own-words/

HARRY'S FLAME Who is Tess Ward? The Naked Diet author and Harry Styles' new girlfriend who's been trolled by One Direction fans
https://www.thesun.co.uk/tvandshowbiz/3509849/tess-ward-naked-diet-harry-styles-girlfriend-blogger/

HARRY STYLE Chart-topper Harry Styles on how his new album was 'therapy', One Direction's future and his sexuality
https://www.thesun.co.uk/tvandshowbiz/3560582/harry-styles-new-album-therapy-flame-tess-ward-dan-wootton-exclusive/

Haz SOLO Harry Styles was Disney bosses' favourite to take on Harrison Ford's iconic Star Wars role before opting for Alden Ehrenreich
https://www.thesun.co.uk/tvandshowbiz/3303100/harry-styles-was-disney-bosses-favourite-to-take-on-harrison-fords-iconic-star-wars-role-before-opting-for-alden-ehrenreich/

BBC
Review: One Direction – What Makes you Beautiful
http://www.bbc.co.uk/newsround/14823863

NME
One Direction – 'What Makes you Beautiful' Review
http://www.nme.com/blogs/nme-blogs/one-direction-what-makes-you-beautiful-review-33888

Daily Record
One Direction star Harry Styles' dad on bond between him and his boy
http://www.dailyrecord.co.uk/entertainment/celebrity/one-direction-star-harry-styles-1130085

Hello
Harry Styles lands new Hollywood acting role
http://www..com/film/2016031430288/harry-styles-new-acting-role/

Vogue
Harry Styles' Style Evolution
http://www.vogue.co.uk/gallery/harry-styles-style-evolution

Sugarscape
Harry Styles' friend Will Sweeny reveals all: 'He can get women, but he's not a womaniser'
http://www.pressparty.com/pg/newsdesk/londonnewsdesk/view/60338/

Entertainment Weekly
One Direction's Harry Styles: 'Soundtrack of My Life'
http://ew.com/article/2015/11/10/one-direction-harry-styles-soundtrack-my-life/

Manchester Evening News
Aiming for stardom: White Eskimo – the Cheshire band Harry Styles left behind for One Direction
http://www.manchestereveningnews.co.uk/whats-on/film-and-tv/aiming-for-stardom-white-eskimo---1210127

REFERENCES

Crewe Chronicle
One Direction star Harry Styles' meteoric rise to fame
http://www.crewechronicle.co.uk/whats-on/music/one-direction-star-harry-styles-5611544

Shropshire Star
X Factor's Liam Payne and Treyc Cohen lift the lid
on show
https://www.shropshirestar.com entertainment/2010/10/16/x-factors-liam-payne-and-treyc-cohen-lift-the-lid-on-show/#b7y13rhf3EddEtjs.99